Strike Deals Like Pro Unleash Your Inner Negotiation Ninja and Command Supplier Success

By mahmoud adel

Copyright © 2024 Author Name: Mahmoud Adel
All rights reserved.
ISBN:

DEDICATION

Insert dedication text here. Insert

dedication text here. Insert
dedication text here. Insert
dedication text here. Insert
dedication text here. Insert
dedication text here. Insert
dedication text here. Insert
dedication text here. Insert
dedication text here. Insert
dedication text here.

Content of table

Strike Deals Like Pro Unleash Your Inner Negotiation Ninja and Command Supplier Success	*i*
Content of table	*6*
Introduction: Unleash Your Inner Negotiation Ninja	*9*
Chapter 1: Understanding Negotiation Psychology	*11*
Chapter 2: The Power of Persuasion	*13*
Chapter 3: Leveraging Influence Techniques	*15*
Chapter 4: Overcoming Cognitive Biases	*17*
Chapter 5: Tactical Manoeuvres: Anchoring and Framing	*19*
Chapter 6: The Art of Mirroring and Matching	*21*
Chapter 7: The Power of Silence	*23*
Chapter 8: Crafting Strategic Concessions	*25*
Chapter 9: Building Rapport and Trust	*27*
Chapter 10: Effective Communication Strategies	*29*
Chapter 11: Preparing for Negotiations: Research and Planning	*32*
Chapter 12: Setting Clear Objectives and Goals	*35*
Chapter 13: Anticipating and Addressing Obstacles	*38*
Chapter 14: Navigating Cultural Differences	*41*
Chapter 15: Embracing Collaborative Negotiation	*44*
Chapter 16: Managing Negotiation Dynamics	*47*
Chapter 17: Leveraging Technology in Negotiations	*50*
Chapter 18: Managing Conflict in Negotiations	*53*
Chapter 19: Overcoming Negotiation Deadlocks	*56*
Chapter 20: Crafting Win-Win Agreements	*59*
Chapter 21: Implementing Effective Follow-Up Strategies	*62*
Chapter 22: Resolving Disputes Amicably	*65*

Chapter 23: Cultivating Long-Term Relationships — 68
Chapter 24: Managing Supplier Performance — 71
Chapter 25: Adapting to Changing Market Conditions — 74
Chapter 26: Leveraging Strategic Alliances — 77
Chapter 27: Sustainable Sourcing Practices — 80
Chapter 28: Ethical Considerations in Supplier Negotiations — 83
Chapter 29: Managing Cultural Differences in Supplier Negotiations — 86
Chapter 30: Crisis Management in Supplier Relationships — 89
Chapter 31: Leveraging Technology in Supplier Negotiations — 92
Chapter 32: Negotiating Sustainable Pricing Models — 95
Chapter 33: Leveraging Negotiation Power Dynamics — 98
Chapter 34: Overcoming Common Negotiation Challenges — 101
Chapter 35: Mastering Contract Negotiation — 104
Chapter 36: Managing Supplier Relationships — 107
Chapter 37: Supplier Performance Management — 110
Chapter 38: Supply Chain Risk Management — 113
Chapter 39: Sustainable Procurement Practices — 116
Chapter 40: Supplier Diversity and Inclusion Initiatives — 119
Chapter 41: Ethical Sourcing and Corporate Social Responsibility — 122
Chapter 42: Conflict Resolution Strategies in Supplier Relationships — 125
Chapter 43: Supplier Performance Improvement Plans — 128
Chapter 44: Leveraging Technology for Supplier Relationship Management — 131
Chapter 45: Future Trends in Supplier Relationship Management — 134
Chapter 46: The Role of Trust in Supplier Relationships — 138

Chapter 47: Cultural Intelligence in Global Supplier Relationships **141**

Chapter 48: The Future of Sustainable Procurement **144**

Chapter 49: Supplier Relationship Governance Frameworks **148**

Chapter 50: Supplier Relationship Exit Strategies **152**

Introduction: Unleash Your Inner Negotiation Ninja

Welcome to "Strike Deals Like A Pro: Unleash Your Inner Negotiation Ninja and Command Supplier Success"! In this eBook, we're embarking on an exciting journey into the art of supplier negotiations. Whether you're a seasoned business professional, an aspiring entrepreneur, a purchasing manager, or a supply chain aficionado, this guide is your ticket to mastering the intricate dance of negotiation.

Negotiation isn't just about haggling over prices or terms; it's a strategic game of influence, psychology, and relationship-building. And in today's competitive business landscape, the ability to negotiate effectively with suppliers can mean the difference between success and stagnation.

In the chapters ahead, we'll delve deep into the psychology behind negotiation, uncover tactical maneuvers to outmaneuver even the savviest suppliers, and explore strategies for building long-lasting, mutually beneficial relationships. From understanding the subtle cues of body language to crafting win-win solutions that leave both parties satisfied, we've got you covered.

But this isn't just theory—we're bringing real-world case studies and practical tips to the table, ensuring that every concept we explore is grounded in actionable advice. Whether you're negotiating multimillion-dollar contracts or hammering out details with local vendors, you'll find valuable insights to elevate your negotiation game to new heights.

So, grab your metaphorical katana, sharpen your instincts, and get ready to unleash your inner negotiation ninja. The journey starts now, and the rewards are limited only by your willingness to learn, adapt, and conquer. Let's dive in and command supplier success like never before!

Chapter 1: Understanding Negotiation Psychology

In the first chapter of "Strike Deals Like A Pro: Unleash Your Inner Negotiation Ninja and Command Supplier Success," we delve into the fascinating world of negotiation psychology. Here, we explore the inner workings of the human mind during negotiations, uncovering the subconscious biases, motivations, and emotions that influence decision-making.

Understanding negotiation psychology is essential for mastering the art of negotiation. By gaining insight into the cognitive processes at play, you'll be better equipped to anticipate and navigate your counterpart's behaviors and responses, ultimately increasing your chances of achieving favorable outcomes.

In this chapter, we'll explore topics such as:

1. The role of perception and interpretation in negotiation dynamics.
2. Common cognitive biases that can affect judgment and decision-making.
3. The influence of emotions on negotiation outcomes and how to manage them effectively.
4. Strategies for building rapport and establishing trust with your negotiating partner.
5. Techniques for uncovering underlying interests and priorities to identify mutually beneficial solutions.

By the end of this chapter, you'll have a solid foundation in negotiation psychology, armed with the knowledge and insights needed to approach negotiations with confidence and finesse. So, sharpen your mental toolkit and get ready to decode the secrets of negotiation psychology as we embark on this transformative journey together.

Chapter 2: The Power of Persuasion

In the second chapter of "Strike Deals Like a Pro: Unleash Your Inner Negotiation Ninja and Command Supplier Success," we delve into the art of persuasion—a critical skill in the negotiation arsenal. Persuasion is the ability to influence others' attitudes, beliefs, and behaviors, and it plays a pivotal role in achieving successful negotiation outcomes.

Throughout this chapter, we'll explore the various techniques and strategies for mastering the power of persuasion in supplier negotiations. Here are some key topics we'll cover:

1. Understanding the principles of persuasion: We'll explore the renowned principles of persuasion, such as reciprocity, scarcity, authority, consistency, liking, and consensus, and how they can be effectively applied in negotiation contexts.

2. Building credibility and authority: Learn how to establish yourself as a credible and authoritative negotiator, gaining your counterpart's respect and trust in the process.
3. Crafting persuasive messages: Discover how to tailor your messages to resonate with your negotiating partner's values, interests, and motivations, increasing the likelihood of agreement and cooperation.
4. Utilizing persuasive language and framing: Explore the power of language and framing in shaping perceptions and influencing decisions during negotiations, and how to use them to your advantage.
5. Overcoming resistance and objections: Develop strategies for overcoming resistance and objections from your counterpart, turning potential roadblocks into opportunities for agreement.

By mastering the art of persuasion, you'll enhance your ability to sway opinions, drive consensus, and ultimately achieve your negotiation objectives with confidence and finesse. So, prepare to unlock the secrets of persuasion and harness its transformative power in your supplier negotiations.

Chapter 3: Leveraging Influence Techniques

Welcome to Chapter 3 of "Strike Deals Like a Pro: Unleash Your Inner Negotiation Ninja and Command Supplier Success." In this chapter, we delve into the realm of influence techniques—the subtle yet powerful strategies for shaping opinions, decisions, and behaviors in negotiation settings.

Here's what you can expect to explore in this chapter:

1. Reciprocity: Discover how the principle of reciprocity can be leveraged to create a sense of obligation and goodwill in your negotiating counterpart, leading to more favorable outcomes.

2. Social proof: Explore the concept of social proof and how you can use it to your advantage by highlighting testimonials, success stories, and endorsements from satisfied customers or partners.
3. Authority: Learn how to establish and communicate your expertise, credentials, and credibility to enhance your influence and persuasion during negotiations.
4. Consistency: Understand the power of consistency and how to use it to gain commitment and agreement from your negotiating partner by aligning with their previous statements or actions.
5. Liking: Explore strategies for building rapport, likability, and trust with your counterpart, increasing their receptivity to your proposals and suggestions.
6. Scarcity: Discover how the principle of scarcity can be used to create a sense of urgency and value in negotiation situations, motivating your counterpart to act quickly and decisively.

Throughout this chapter, we'll delve into real-world examples, case studies, and practical

exercises to help you master these influence techniques and apply them effectively in your supplier negotiations. By leveraging the power of influence, you'll be able to steer conversations, shape perceptions, and ultimately achieve your negotiation goals with finesse and confidence. So, let's dive in and uncover the secrets of influence together!

Chapter 4: Overcoming Cognitive Biases

Welcome to Chapter 4 of "Strike Deals Like a Pro: Unleash Your Inner Negotiation Ninja and Command Supplier Success." In this chapter, we'll explore the fascinating world of cognitive biases—deep-seated mental shortcuts and patterns of thinking that can influence decision-making in negotiation settings.

Here's what we'll cover in this chapter:

1. Understanding cognitive biases: Dive into the various cognitive biases that can

impact negotiation outcomes, such as confirmation bias, anchoring bias, availability bias, and overconfidence bias.
2. Recognizing cognitive biases in yourself and others: Learn how to identify cognitive biases in your own thinking and behavior, as well as in your negotiating counterpart, to avoid falling victim to their influence.
3. Mitigating the effects of cognitive biases: Discover strategies for mitigating the effects of cognitive biases in negotiation, such as slowing down decision-making processes, seeking diverse perspectives, and conducting thorough analysis.
4. Leveraging cognitive biases strategically: Explore how you can use knowledge of cognitive biases to your advantage in negotiation, such as by framing proposals in a way that exploits anchoring bias or presenting options to counteract confirmation bias.
5. Building decision-making resilience: Develop resilience against cognitive biases by cultivating awareness, critical thinking skills, and emotional intelligence, allowing

you to make more rational and strategic decisions in negotiation.

By understanding and effectively navigating cognitive biases, you'll be better equipped to approach negotiations with clarity, insight, and strategic acumen. So, let's dive into the fascinating world of cognitive biases and uncover the secrets to overcoming their influence in supplier negotiations.

Chapter 5: Tactical Manoeuvres: Anchoring and Framing

Welcome to Chapter 5 of "Strike Deals Like a Pro: Unleash Your Inner Negotiation Ninja and Command Supplier Success." In this chapter, we'll explore two powerful tactical maneuvers—anchoring and framing—that can significantly impact negotiation outcomes.

Here's what we'll delve into in this chapter:

1. Understanding anchoring: Explore the concept of anchoring and how it involves the initial information or offer presented in a

negotiation setting, influencing subsequent discussions and outcomes.
2. Utilizing anchoring to your advantage: Learn how to strategically set anchors in negotiation by presenting initial offers, price points, or terms that shape your counterpart's perception of value and acceptable terms.
3. Overcoming anchoring effects: Discover strategies for overcoming the influence of anchors set by your negotiating counterpart, such as by reframing the discussion, providing counterarguments, or introducing new information.
4. Exploring framing techniques: Dive into the art of framing and how it involves presenting information in a way that shapes perceptions, preferences, and decisions in negotiation.
5. Crafting persuasive frames: Explore strategies for crafting persuasive frames that highlight the benefits, advantages, and value of your proposals, increasing your counterpart's receptivity and agreement.
6. Responding to framing attempts: Learn how to identify and respond to framing attempts by your negotiating counterpart, leveraging counter frames to shift the discussion in your favor.

Throughout this chapter, we'll examine real-world examples, case studies, and practical exercises to help you master anchoring and framing techniques and apply them effectively in your supplier negotiations. By mastering these tactical maneuvers, you'll be able to shape perceptions, steer discussions, and ultimately achieve your negotiation objectives with finesse and confidence. So, let's dive in and uncover the secrets to anchoring and framing success!

Chapter 6: The Art of Mirroring and Matching

Welcome to Chapter 6 of "Strike Deals Like a Pro: Unleash Your Inner Negotiation Ninja and Command Supplier Success." In this chapter, we'll explore the subtle yet powerful technique of mirroring and matching, a skillful method for building rapport and establishing connection with your negotiating counterpart.

Here's what we'll cover in this chapter:

1. Understanding mirroring and matching: Delve into the concept of mirroring and matching, which involves subtly mimicking the body language, vocal tone, and communication style of your counterpart to create a sense of familiarity and rapport.
2. Building rapport through nonverbal cues: Learn how to observe and replicate your counterpart's nonverbal cues, such as posture, gestures, facial expressions, and pacing, to establish a deeper connection and build trust.
3. Matching verbal communication: Explore techniques for matching your counterpart's verbal communication style, including tone, tempo, vocabulary, and level of formality, to enhance rapport and alignment.
4. Mirroring emotions and energy: Discover how to mirror your counterpart's emotions and energy levels during negotiation, creating a sense of empathy, understanding, and collaboration.
5. Maintaining authenticity: Learn how to balance mirroring and matching techniques with authenticity, ensuring that your gestures and expressions remain genuine and sincere.
6. Leveraging mirroring and matching strategically: Explore how mirroring and matching can be used strategically to

influence your counterpart's behavior, build rapport, and create a more cooperative negotiation environment.

Throughout this chapter, we'll delve into real-world examples, case studies, and practical exercises to help you master the art of mirroring and matching and apply it effectively in your supplier negotiations. By honing your ability to connect with your negotiating counterpart on a deeper level, you'll enhance trust, collaboration, and ultimately achieve more successful negotiation outcomes. So, let's dive in and uncover the secrets to mastering mirroring and matching in negotiation!

Chapter 7: The Power of Silence

Welcome to Chapter 7 of "Strike Deals Like a Pro: Unleash Your Inner Negotiation Ninja and Command Supplier Success." In this chapter, we'll explore the often underestimated yet incredibly powerful tactic of silence in negotiation.

Here's what we'll delve into in this chapter:

1. Understanding the role of silence: Explore the significance of silence as a strategic tool in negotiation, capable of conveying power, confidence, and control.
2. Harnessing the power of pause: Learn how to use strategic pauses during negotiation to your advantage, allowing you to gather your thoughts, observe your counterpart's reactions, and assert your position without saying a word.
3. Creating discomfort: Discover how silence can create discomfort and uncertainty for your counterpart, prompting them to reveal more information, make concessions, or become more receptive to your proposals.
4. Listening and observing: Explore how silence can encourage your counterpart to speak more freely, share additional insights, and reveal their true intentions, allowing you to gain valuable information and insights.
5. Using silence as a negotiation tactic: Learn how to strategically deploy silence as a negotiation tactic, such as in response to offers, proposals, or requests, to create leverage and influence the direction of the discussion.
6. Managing your emotions: Discover techniques for managing your emotions

during moments of silence, maintaining composure, and resisting the urge to break the silence prematurely.

Throughout this chapter, we'll examine real-world examples, case studies, and practical exercises to help you master the art of using silence in negotiation effectively. By embracing the power of silence, you'll enhance your ability to control the pace, direction, and outcomes of negotiations, ultimately achieving greater success in your supplier relationships. So, let's dive in and uncover the secrets to harnessing the power of silence like a negotiation ninja!

Chapter 8: Crafting Strategic Concessions

Welcome to Chapter 8 of "Strike Deals Like a Pro: Unleash Your Inner Negotiation Ninja and Command Supplier Success." In this chapter, we'll explore the art of crafting strategic concessions in negotiation, a key skill for achieving mutually beneficial outcomes while maintaining control and maximizing value.

Here's what we'll cover in this chapter:

1. Understanding concessions: Delve into the concept of concessions in negotiation and how they involve making compromises or trade-offs to move negotiations forward and reach agreement.
2. Identifying your priorities: Learn how to identify and prioritize your interests, goals, and non-negotiables in negotiation, allowing you to focus your concessions strategically and protect your most valuable assets.
3. Strategic concession planning: Explore techniques for planning and strategizing your concessions in advance, considering factors such as your counterpart's priorities, leverage, and potential areas for compromise.
4. Trading concessions: Discover how to effectively trade concessions with your negotiating counterpart, seeking to maximize value and achieve win-win outcomes that satisfy both parties' interests.
5. Concession management: Learn strategies for managing concessions throughout the negotiation process, including knowing when

to concede, how much to concede, and how to communicate concessions effectively.
6. Leveraging concessions for leverage: Explore how concessions can be used strategically to create leverage, build trust, and influence your counterpart's behavior and decisions.

Throughout this chapter, we'll delve into real-world examples, case studies, and practical exercises to help you master the art of crafting strategic concessions in negotiation. By honing your ability to make concessions strategically, you'll enhance your negotiation effectiveness, build stronger relationships with your suppliers, and achieve greater success in your business endeavors. So, let's dive in and uncover the secrets to crafting concessions like a negotiation ninja!

Chapter 9: Building Rapport and Trust

Welcome to Chapter 9 of "Strike Deals Like a Pro: Unleash Your Inner Negotiation Ninja and Command Supplier Success." In this chapter, we'll explore the critical importance of building rapport and trust in negotiation, and how these elements can significantly influence the outcomes of your interactions with suppliers.

Here's what we'll delve into in this chapter:

1. The foundation of rapport and trust: Understand the fundamental concepts of rapport and trust and how they serve as the bedrock of successful negotiations. We'll explore why establishing a positive relationship with your counterpart is essential for achieving mutually beneficial outcomes.
2. Establishing rapport: Learn strategies for establishing rapport with your negotiating counterpart, including active listening, empathy, genuine interest, and finding common ground. We'll also discuss the importance of nonverbal communication in building rapport.
3. Building trust: Explore techniques for building trust with your suppliers, such as transparency, integrity, consistency, and reliability. We'll discuss how demonstrating trustworthiness can foster cooperation, openness, and collaboration in negotiations.
4. Handling trust barriers: Identify common barriers to trust in negotiation, such as skepticism, past experiences, and cultural differences, and learn how to overcome them effectively. We'll discuss

strategies for addressing trust issues and rebuilding trust when it has been compromised.
5. Repairing damaged rapport and trust: Discover strategies for repairing damaged rapport and trust in negotiation, including acknowledging mistakes, apologizing sincerely, and demonstrating commitment to rebuilding the relationship.
6. Maintaining rapport and trust: Learn how to maintain rapport and trust throughout the negotiation process and beyond, including staying true to your word, following through on commitments, and fostering a positive working relationship with your suppliers.

Throughout this chapter, we'll explore real-world examples, case studies, and practical exercises to help you master the art of building rapport and trust in negotiation. By cultivating strong relationships with your suppliers based on trust and mutual respect, you'll enhance your negotiation effectiveness, foster cooperation, and achieve greater success in your business endeavors. So, let's dive in and uncover the secrets to building rapport and trust like a negotiation ninja!

Chapter 10: Effective Communication Strategies

Welcome to Chapter 10 of "Strike Deals Like a Pro: Unleash Your Inner Negotiation Ninja and Command Supplier Success." In this chapter, we'll explore the critical role of effective communication in negotiation and how mastering communication strategies can enhance your ability to achieve successful outcomes with suppliers.

Here's what we'll cover in this chapter:

1. The importance of communication in negotiation: Understand why effective communication is essential for building rapport, conveying information, and influencing outcomes in negotiation. We'll explore the impact of communication styles, clarity, and transparency on negotiation dynamics.
2. Active listening techniques: Learn how to become a better listener during negotiations, including techniques such as

paraphrasing, clarifying, and summarizing. We'll discuss the importance of listening for both verbal and nonverbal cues to gain insights into your counterpart's perspectives and interests.
3. Assertive communication: Explore strategies for assertive communication in negotiation, including expressing your needs, preferences, and boundaries confidently and respectfully. We'll discuss how assertiveness can help you advocate for your interests while maintaining positive relationships with suppliers.
4. Clarifying and confirming understanding: Discover techniques for clarifying and confirming understanding during negotiations to ensure alignment and avoid misunderstandings. We'll discuss the importance of asking clarifying questions, summarizing key points, and seeking feedback to verify comprehension.
5. Managing emotions and conflict: Learn how to manage emotions and conflict effectively in negotiation, including techniques for staying calm under

pressure, de-escalating tense situations, and finding mutually acceptable solutions. We'll discuss the role of emotional intelligence in navigating challenging negotiation dynamics.
6. Tailoring communication to cultural differences: Explore how cultural differences can impact communication in negotiation and learn strategies for adapting your communication style to accommodate diverse cultural norms and preferences. We'll discuss the importance of cultural sensitivity and awareness in building rapport and trust with suppliers from different cultural backgrounds.

Throughout this chapter, we'll explore real-world examples, case studies, and practical exercises to help you master effective communication strategies in negotiation. By honing your communication skills, you'll enhance your ability to convey your message, understand your counterpart's perspectives, and ultimately achieve successful outcomes in your supplier negotiations. So, let's dive in and uncover the secrets to effective communication like a negotiation ninja!

Chapter 11: Preparing for Negotiations: Research and Planning

Welcome to Chapter 11 of "Strike Deals Like a Pro: Unleash Your Inner Negotiation Ninja and Command Supplier Success." In this chapter, we'll explore the critical steps involved in preparing for negotiations, emphasizing the importance of thorough research and strategic planning.

Here's what we'll delve into in this chapter:

1. Understanding the importance of preparation: Explore why thorough preparation is essential for successful negotiations, including the impact of preparation on confidence, clarity, and negotiation outcomes.

2. Setting clear objectives and goals: Learn how to define clear objectives and goals for your negotiations, including desired outcomes, priorities, and potential trade-offs. We'll discuss the importance of aligning your negotiation objectives with your organization's broader strategic objectives.
3. Conducting comprehensive research: Discover techniques for conducting comprehensive research before negotiations, including gathering information about your counterpart, their business, industry trends, market conditions, and competitive landscape. We'll explore the role of research in uncovering potential areas of leverage, opportunities, and risks.
4. Analyzing BATNA and WATNA: Learn how to analyze your Best Alternative to a Negotiated Agreement (BATNA) and Worst Alternative to a Negotiated Agreement (WATNA) to assess your negotiation leverage and identify your walk-away points. We'll discuss strategies for maximizing your BATNA and minimizing

your WATNA to strengthen your negotiating position.
5. Anticipating and addressing obstacles: Explore techniques for anticipating potential obstacles and challenges in negotiations, including cultural differences, communication barriers, and resistance from your counterpart. We'll discuss strategies for proactively addressing obstacles and developing contingency plans to overcome them.
6. Developing a negotiation strategy: Learn how to develop a negotiation strategy tailored to your specific objectives, priorities, and circumstances. We'll discuss different negotiation approaches, such as distributive (competitive) and integrative (collaborative) negotiation, and how to adapt your strategy based on the dynamics of each negotiation situation.

Throughout this chapter, we'll explore real-world examples, case studies, and practical exercises to help you master the art of preparing for negotiations effectively. By investing time and effort in thorough research and strategic planning, you'll enhance your negotiation readiness, confidence, and ultimately achieve better outcomes in your supplier negotiations. So, let's dive in and uncover the secrets to negotiation preparation like a negotiation ninja!

Chapter 12: Setting Clear Objectives and Goals

Welcome to Chapter 12 of "Strike Deals Like a Pro: Unleash Your Inner Negotiation Ninja and Command Supplier Success." In this chapter, we'll delve into the crucial process of setting clear objectives and goals for your negotiations, laying the foundation for success.

Here's what we'll explore in this chapter:

1. Understanding the importance of clear objectives: Learn why setting clear objectives is essential for guiding your

negotiation strategy, maintaining focus, and measuring success. We'll discuss how well-defined objectives help you prioritize issues, allocate resources effectively, and stay aligned with your organization's broader goals.
2. Defining SMART objectives: Discover the SMART framework for setting objectives—Specific, Measurable, Achievable, Relevant, and Time-bound—and how to apply it to your negotiation goals. We'll explore techniques for ensuring that your objectives are clear, realistic, and actionable.
3. Identifying key priorities: Learn how to identify and prioritize your key priorities for negotiation, considering factors such as value, importance, urgency, and strategic significance. We'll discuss techniques for distinguishing between must-have, nice-to-have, and non-negotiable priorities to focus your efforts effectively.
4. Clarifying desired outcomes: Explore techniques for clarifying your desired outcomes for negotiation, including

specific targets, benchmarks, and performance indicators. We'll discuss the importance of aligning your desired outcomes with your organization's broader objectives and stakeholder expectations.
5. Considering potential trade-offs: Discover how to anticipate potential trade-offs and concessions that may arise during negotiations and how to prepare accordingly. We'll discuss techniques for evaluating trade-offs based on their impact on your objectives and priorities, as well as strategies for maximizing value while minimizing concessions.
6. Communicating objectives effectively: Learn how to communicate your objectives clearly and persuasively to your negotiating counterpart, building alignment and buy-in. We'll explore techniques for framing your objectives in a way that resonates with your counterpart's interests and motivations, fostering a collaborative negotiation environment.

Throughout this chapter, we'll delve into real-world examples, case studies, and practical

exercises to help you master the art of setting clear objectives and goals for your negotiations. By defining your objectives with precision and clarity, you'll enhance your negotiation effectiveness, focus, and ultimately achieve better outcomes in your supplier negotiations. So, let's dive in and uncover the secrets to setting objectives like a negotiation ninja!

Chapter 13: Anticipating and Addressing Obstacles

Welcome to Chapter 13 of "Strike Deals Like a Pro: Unleash Your Inner Negotiation Ninja and Command Supplier Success." In this chapter, we'll explore the critical process of anticipating and addressing obstacles that may arise during negotiations, ensuring smoother and more successful outcomes.

Here's what we'll cover in this chapter:

1. Understanding negotiation obstacles: Delve into common obstacles and challenges that may arise during negotiations, such as resistance from your counterpart, cultural differences, communication barriers, and unforeseen circumstances. We'll explore how these obstacles can impact negotiation dynamics and outcomes.
2. Anticipating potential obstacles: Learn how to proactively anticipate potential obstacles before entering into negotiations, based on factors such as your counterpart's behavior, industry norms, past experiences, and external factors. We'll discuss techniques for conducting risk assessments and scenario planning to identify potential challenges.
3. Developing contingency plans: Discover strategies for developing contingency plans to address potential obstacles and mitigate their impact on negotiation outcomes. We'll discuss techniques for identifying alternative approaches, fallback options, and exit strategies to navigate obstacles effectively.

4. Building flexibility and adaptability: Explore the importance of building flexibility and adaptability into your negotiation approach, allowing you to respond effectively to unexpected obstacles and changing circumstances. We'll discuss techniques for staying agile and adjusting your strategy in real-time to overcome obstacles as they arise.
5. Leveraging creativity and innovation: Learn how to leverage creativity and innovation to overcome obstacles creatively and find mutually beneficial solutions. We'll explore techniques for brainstorming alternative options, reframing challenges as opportunities, and thinking outside the box to break through impasses.
6. Seeking collaboration and support: Discover how to leverage collaboration and support from internal and external stakeholders to address obstacles collaboratively. We'll discuss techniques for building consensus, rallying support, and leveraging resources to overcome challenges effectively.

Throughout this chapter, we'll delve into real-world examples, case studies, and practical exercises to help you master the art of anticipating and addressing obstacles in negotiation. By proactively identifying and navigating obstacles, you'll enhance your negotiation effectiveness, resilience, and ultimately achieve better outcomes in your supplier negotiations. So, let's dive in and uncover the secrets to overcoming obstacles like a negotiation ninja!

Chapter 14: Navigating Cultural Differences

Welcome to Chapter 14 of "Strike Deals Like a Pro: Unleash Your Inner Negotiation Ninja and Command Supplier Success." In this chapter, we'll explore the intricate process of navigating cultural differences in negotiations, a critical skill in today's global business environment.

Here's what we'll delve into in this chapter:

1. Understanding cultural dimensions: Explore the concept of cultural dimensions, such as Hofstede's cultural dimensions theory, and how they shape communication styles, decision-making processes, and negotiation behaviors across different cultures.
2. Recognizing cultural differences: Learn how to recognize and appreciate cultural differences in negotiation, including differences in communication norms, attitudes toward risk, concepts of time, and approaches to conflict resolution.
3. Adapting your negotiation approach: Discover strategies for adapting your negotiation approach to accommodate cultural differences effectively. We'll discuss techniques for building rapport, demonstrating respect, and adjusting your communication style to align with your counterpart's cultural preferences.
4. Building cultural intelligence: Explore the concept of cultural intelligence (CQ) and

how to develop your cultural awareness, understanding, and sensitivity in negotiation contexts. We'll discuss techniques for learning about different cultures, seeking feedback, and reflecting on your own cultural biases.

5. Overcoming cultural barriers: Learn how to overcome cultural barriers and misunderstandings that may arise during negotiations, such as language barriers, misinterpretations, and stereotypes. We'll discuss techniques for building trust, clarifying intentions, and fostering open communication across cultures.

6. Leveraging cultural diversity: Discover how to leverage cultural diversity as a strength in negotiation, drawing on the unique perspectives, insights, and skills of individuals from different cultural backgrounds. We'll explore techniques for harnessing diversity to drive creativity, innovation, and better decision-making in negotiations.

Throughout this chapter, we'll delve into real-world examples, case studies, and practical exercises to help you master the art of navigating cultural differences in negotiation. By developing your cultural intelligence and adapting your approach accordingly, you'll enhance your negotiation effectiveness, build stronger relationships with your suppliers, and achieve better outcomes in your business endeavors. So, let's dive in and uncover the secrets to navigating cultural differences like a negotiation ninja!

Chapter 15: Embracing Collaborative Negotiation

Welcome to Chapter 15 of "Strike Deals Like a Pro: Unleash Your Inner Negotiation Ninja and Command Supplier Success." In this chapter, we'll explore the principles and strategies of collaborative negotiation, where parties work together to create value and maximize outcomes for mutual benefit.

Here's what we'll cover in this chapter:

1. Understanding collaborative negotiation: Delve into the concept of collaborative negotiation, also known as integrative negotiation or win-win negotiation. Learn how this approach differs from competitive negotiation and why it's beneficial for building long-term relationships and creating sustainable agreements.
2. Building trust and rapport: Explore how building trust and rapport with your negotiating counterpart is essential for fostering a collaborative negotiation environment. We'll discuss techniques for establishing common ground, demonstrating empathy, and focusing on shared interests.
3. Identifying shared interests: Learn how to identify and prioritize shared interests—areas where both parties' objectives overlap or align. Discover techniques for uncovering underlying needs, goals, and values that can serve as the basis for collaborative problem-solving and value creation.

4. Brainstorming and creative problem-solving: Discover how to leverage brainstorming and creative problem-solving techniques to generate innovative solutions that satisfy both parties' interests. We'll explore techniques such as lateral thinking, reframing, and exploring multiple options to find mutually beneficial agreements.
5. Negotiating value instead of positions: Shift your focus from negotiating fixed positions to negotiating value—finding ways to expand the pie and create additional value for both parties. Learn how to explore trade-offs, package deals, and explore creative solutions that maximize joint gains.
6. Building win-win agreements: Explore strategies for building win-win agreements that address both parties' interests and concerns. We'll discuss techniques for structuring agreements, drafting clear terms, and ensuring accountability to maintain trust and commitment.

Throughout this chapter, we'll delve into real-world examples, case studies, and practical exercises to help you master the principles and strategies of collaborative negotiation. By embracing collaborative negotiation approaches, you'll enhance your negotiation effectiveness, build stronger relationships with your suppliers, and achieve better outcomes in your business endeavors. So, let's dive in and uncover the secrets to embracing collaborative negotiation like a negotiation ninja!

Chapter 16: Managing Negotiation Dynamics

Welcome to Chapter 16 of "Strike Deals Like a Pro: Unleash Your Inner Negotiation Ninja and Command Supplier Success." In this chapter, we'll explore the intricacies of managing negotiation dynamics—understanding the various factors and forces at play that influence the outcome of negotiations.

Here's what we'll delve into in this chapter:

1. Dynamics of power: Understand the concept of power in negotiation and how it manifests through factors such as resources, expertise, alternatives, and leverage. Learn how to assess power dynamics and navigate power imbalances effectively to achieve favorable outcomes.
2. Balancing assertiveness and empathy: Explore the delicate balance between assertiveness and empathy in negotiation, understanding when to assert your interests and when to demonstrate empathy toward your counterpart's concerns. Discover techniques for maintaining a collaborative negotiation environment while advocating for your interests.
3. Managing emotions: Learn how to manage emotions—both your own and your counterpart's—during negotiations. Discover techniques for staying calm under pressure, de-escalating tense situations, and diffusing emotional conflicts to keep negotiations on track.

4. Handling impasses and deadlocks: Explore strategies for handling impasses and deadlocks in negotiation, where parties reach a stalemate or struggle to make progress. Learn techniques for reframing issues, introducing new options, and seeking assistance from mediators or third parties to break through impasses.
5. Adapting to changing circumstances: Discover how to adapt your negotiation approach to changing circumstances, such as new information, shifts in market conditions, or unexpected developments. Learn techniques for staying agile and adjusting your strategy in real-time to maximize outcomes.
6. Closing the deal: Explore strategies for effectively closing the deal and reaching agreement with your counterpart. Learn techniques for summarizing key points, clarifying terms, and obtaining commitment to ensure a successful conclusion to negotiations.

Throughout this chapter, we'll delve into real-world examples, case studies, and practical

exercises to help you master the art of managing negotiation dynamics effectively. By understanding and navigating the various forces at play in negotiations, you'll enhance your negotiation effectiveness, build stronger relationships with your suppliers, and achieve better outcomes in your business endeavors. So, let's dive in and uncover the secrets to managing negotiation dynamics like a negotiation ninja!

Chapter 17: Leveraging Technology in Negotiations

Welcome to Chapter 17 of "Strike Deals Like a Pro: Unleash Your Inner Negotiation Ninja and Command Supplier Success." In this chapter, we'll explore the increasingly important role of technology in modern negotiations and how you can leverage it to enhance your negotiation effectiveness.

Here's what we'll cover in this chapter:

1. The digital landscape of negotiations: Understand how technology has transformed the negotiation landscape, from virtual communication tools to digital platforms for document sharing, collaboration, and decision-making.
2. Virtual negotiation platforms: Explore the use of virtual negotiation platforms, such as video conferencing software and online meeting platforms, for conducting negotiations remotely. Learn how to leverage features like screen sharing, chat, and virtual whiteboards to facilitate communication and collaboration.
3. Document management systems: Discover the benefits of document management systems for organizing, sharing, and collaborating on negotiation-related documents and agreements. Learn how cloud-based storage solutions and version control tools can streamline the negotiation process and ensure accuracy and compliance.

4. Data analytics and insights: Explore how data analytics and insights can inform negotiation strategy and decision-making. Learn how to leverage data visualization tools, predictive analytics, and market intelligence platforms to gain valuable insights into your counterpart's preferences, behaviors, and market trends.
5. AI-powered negotiation assistants: Discover the emerging trend of AI-powered negotiation assistants, which use natural language processing and machine learning algorithms to analyze negotiation data, provide real-time guidance, and generate personalized recommendations. Learn how to leverage these tools to augment your negotiation skills and decision-making capabilities.
6. Security and privacy considerations: Understand the importance of security and privacy in negotiation technology, particularly when dealing with sensitive information and confidential agreements. Learn how to safeguard your data and communications through encryption,

access controls, and secure authentication mechanisms.

Throughout this chapter, we'll delve into real-world examples, case studies, and practical tips to help you leverage technology effectively in your negotiations. By embracing digital tools and platforms, you'll enhance your negotiation efficiency, collaboration, and ultimately achieve better outcomes in your supplier negotiations. So, let's dive in and uncover the secrets to leveraging technology like a negotiation ninja!

Chapter 18: Managing Conflict in Negotiations

Welcome to Chapter 18 of "Strike Deals Like a Pro: Unleash Your Inner Negotiation Ninja and Command Supplier Success." In this chapter, we'll explore the challenging yet inevitable aspect of managing conflict in negotiations and how to navigate it effectively to achieve successful outcomes.

Here's what we'll cover in this chapter:

1. Understanding conflict in negotiations: Delve into the nature of conflict in negotiations and why it often arises due to differences in interests, values, priorities, or communication styles. Learn how to recognize the signs of conflict and its potential impact on negotiation dynamics.
2. Constructive vs. destructive conflict: Explore the difference between constructive conflict, which can lead to innovation, creativity, and better outcomes, and destructive conflict, which can derail negotiations and damage relationships. Learn how to channel conflict productively and minimize its negative effects.
3. Strategies for conflict resolution: Discover techniques for resolving conflict in negotiations, including principled negotiation, interest-based bargaining, and problem-solving approaches. Learn how to separate people from the problem, focus on interests rather than positions, and explore mutually acceptable solutions.

4. Active listening and empathy: Explore the role of active listening and empathy in managing conflict effectively. Learn how to listen actively to your counterpart's concerns, demonstrate empathy for their perspective, and build rapport to facilitate constructive dialogue and problem-solving.
5. De-escalation techniques: Discover strategies for de-escalating conflict and reducing tension in negotiations. Learn techniques for staying calm under pressure, reframing issues positively, and seeking common ground to defuse conflicts and promote collaboration.
6. Seeking third-party assistance: Explore the option of seeking third-party assistance, such as mediators, facilitators, or arbitrators, to help manage conflict and facilitate resolution. Learn how to identify qualified professionals and engage them impartially to support negotiations.

Throughout this chapter, we'll delve into real-world examples, case studies, and practical exercises to help you master the art of managing conflict in negotiations. By understanding the nature of conflict, adopting constructive approaches to resolution, and fostering open communication, you'll enhance your negotiation effectiveness, build stronger relationships with your suppliers, and achieve better outcomes in your business endeavors. So, let's dive in and uncover the secrets to managing conflict like a negotiation ninja!

Chapter 19: Overcoming Negotiation Deadlocks

Welcome to Chapter 19 of "Strike Deals Like a Pro: Unleash Your Inner Negotiation Ninja and Command Supplier Success." In this chapter, we'll explore strategies for overcoming negotiation deadlocks—those challenging situations where parties reach an impasse and struggle to make progress.

Here's what we'll cover in this chapter:

1. Understanding negotiation deadlocks: Delve into the concept of negotiation deadlocks and why they occur, including factors such as conflicting interests, entrenched positions, communication breakdowns, and lack of trust.
2. Identifying the root causes: Learn how to identify the underlying root causes of negotiation deadlocks, such as incompatible goals, misunderstandings, or emotional barriers. Discover techniques for conducting a thorough analysis of the situation to pinpoint the reasons for the impasse.
3. Breaking through impasses: Explore strategies for breaking through negotiation deadlocks and getting negotiations back on track. Learn techniques for reframing issues, exploring creative solutions, and introducing new options to overcome entrenched positions and find common ground.
4. Building bridges: Discover how to build bridges between parties in negotiation

deadlocks, fostering trust, understanding, and collaboration. Learn techniques for building rapport, demonstrating empathy, and finding shared interests to create a foundation for agreement.
5. Seeking alternative perspectives: Explore the value of seeking alternative perspectives and outside opinions to overcome negotiation deadlocks. Learn how to engage neutral third parties, brainstorm with colleagues, or consult experts to gain fresh insights and identify new approaches.
6. Knowing when to walk away: Understand the importance of knowing when to walk away from a negotiation deadlock. Learn how to assess your Best Alternative to a Negotiated Agreement (BATNA) and determine whether it's in your best interest to pursue other options or disengage from the negotiation entirely.

Throughout this chapter, we'll delve into real-world examples, case studies, and practical exercises to help you master the art of overcoming negotiation deadlocks. By understanding the root causes of deadlocks, adopting creative problem-solving approaches, and knowing when to pivot or disengage, you'll enhance your negotiation effectiveness and achieve better outcomes in your supplier negotiations. So, let's dive in and uncover the secrets to overcoming deadlocks like a negotiation ninja!

Chapter 20: Crafting Win-Win Agreements

Welcome to Chapter 20 of "Strike Deals Like a Pro: Unleash Your Inner Negotiation Ninja and Command Supplier Success." In this chapter, we'll explore the art of crafting win-win agreements that satisfy the interests of all parties involved and lay the foundation for successful long-term relationships.

Here's what we'll cover in this chapter:

1. Understanding win-win negotiation: Delve into the principles of win-win negotiation,

where parties collaborate to create value and maximize outcomes for mutual benefit. Learn how win-win agreements focus on addressing underlying interests rather than just reaching a compromise.
2. Identifying shared interests: Explore techniques for identifying shared interests and priorities that form the basis for win-win agreements. Learn how to uncover underlying needs, goals, and values that can be addressed through creative problem-solving and value creation.
3. Maximizing joint gains: Discover strategies for maximizing joint gains in negotiation, where both parties benefit from the agreement. Learn how to explore trade-offs, package deals, and innovative solutions that expand the pie and create value beyond initial expectations.
4. Balancing concessions: Explore techniques for balancing concessions in win-win agreements, ensuring that both parties make meaningful contributions to the final outcome. Learn how to prioritize interests,

evaluate trade-offs, and negotiate terms that satisfy both parties' needs.
5. Building trust and commitment: Understand the importance of building trust and commitment in win-win agreements, fostering a collaborative negotiation environment where parties feel confident in their ability to deliver on their promises. Learn techniques for establishing clear expectations, communicating openly, and following through on commitments.
6. Structuring the agreement: Explore strategies for structuring win-win agreements to ensure clarity, completeness, and enforceability. Learn how to document key terms, address contingencies, and establish mechanisms for resolving disputes or addressing unforeseen circumstances.

Throughout this chapter, we'll delve into real-world examples, case studies, and practical exercises to help you master the art of crafting win-win agreements. By embracing win-win negotiation principles and focusing on creating value for all parties involved, you'll enhance your negotiation effectiveness, build stronger relationships with your suppliers, and achieve better outcomes in your business endeavors. So, let's dive in and uncover the secrets to crafting win-win agreements like a negotiation ninja!

Chapter 21: Implementing Effective Follow-Up Strategies

Welcome to Chapter 21 of "Strike Deals Like a Pro: Unleash Your Inner Negotiation Ninja and Command Supplier Success." In this chapter, we'll explore the importance of implementing effective follow-up strategies after reaching an agreement in negotiations to ensure successful implementation and long-term relationship building.

Here's what we'll cover in this chapter:

1. Importance of follow-up: Understand why follow-up is crucial after reaching an agreement in negotiations. Learn how effective follow-up can help ensure that both parties fulfill their commitments, address any outstanding issues, and maintain the momentum of the negotiation process.
2. Establishing clear expectations: Explore techniques for establishing clear expectations and responsibilities for both parties following the negotiation. Learn how to document key terms, timelines, and deliverables to avoid misunderstandings and ensure accountability.
3. Communication channels: Discover strategies for establishing effective communication channels for post-negotiation follow-up. Learn how to stay in regular contact with your counterpart, provide updates on progress, and address any concerns or issues that may arise.
4. Monitoring and tracking progress: Explore techniques for monitoring and tracking progress towards implementation of the agreement. Learn how to set milestones,

track key performance indicators, and identify any deviations from the agreed-upon plan.
5. Addressing challenges and obstacles: Understand how to proactively address challenges and obstacles that may arise during the implementation phase. Learn techniques for problem-solving, resource allocation, and seeking assistance from stakeholders or third parties as needed.
6. Review and evaluation: Explore the importance of conducting regular reviews and evaluations of the agreement's implementation. Learn how to assess performance, gather feedback from stakeholders, and identify opportunities for improvement or optimization.

Throughout this chapter, we'll delve into real-world examples, case studies, and practical exercises to help you master the art of implementing effective follow-up strategies in negotiation. By staying engaged, proactive, and communicative during the post-negotiation phase, you'll enhance your ability to build trust, maintain relationships, and achieve successful outcomes in your business endeavors. So, let's dive in and uncover the secrets to effective follow-up like a negotiation ninja!

Chapter 22: Resolving Disputes Amicably

Welcome to Chapter 22 of "Strike Deals Like a Pro: Unleash Your Inner Negotiation Ninja and Command Supplier Success." In this chapter, we'll explore the art of resolving disputes amicably in negotiation, focusing on techniques for addressing conflicts and disagreements in a constructive manner.

Here's what we'll cover in this chapter:

1. Understanding dispute resolution: Delve into the concept of dispute resolution in negotiation and why it's essential for maintaining positive relationships and achieving mutually beneficial outcomes. Learn about different approaches to dispute resolution, including negotiation, mediation, arbitration, and litigation.
2. Early intervention: Explore the importance of early intervention in resolving disputes before they escalate. Learn techniques for identifying potential conflicts, addressing concerns, and facilitating open dialogue to prevent disagreements from derailing the negotiation process.
3. Active listening and empathy: Discover how active listening and empathy can help defuse conflicts and foster understanding between parties. Learn techniques for listening attentively to your counterpart's

concerns, acknowledging their perspective, and finding common ground to build rapport.
4. Collaborative problem-solving: Explore the principles of collaborative problem-solving and how it can be applied to resolve disputes in negotiation. Learn techniques for brainstorming solutions, exploring trade-offs, and finding creative alternatives that satisfy both parties' interests.
5. Mediation and third-party intervention: Understand the role of mediation and third-party intervention in resolving disputes amicably. Learn how to engage a neutral mediator or facilitator to help parties communicate effectively, clarify issues, and generate mutually acceptable solutions.
6. Negotiating win-win resolutions: Explore strategies for negotiating win-win resolutions to disputes, where both parties feel satisfied with the outcome. Learn techniques for reframing issues, exploring interests, and finding innovative solutions that address underlying concerns and build trust.

Throughout this chapter, we'll delve into real-world examples, case studies, and practical exercises to help you master the art of resolving disputes amicably in negotiation. By adopting a collaborative and solution-oriented approach to conflict resolution, you'll enhance your negotiation effectiveness, build stronger relationships with your suppliers, and achieve better outcomes in your business endeavors. So, let's dive in and uncover the secrets to resolving disputes like a negotiation ninja!

Chapter 23: Cultivating Long-Term Relationships

Welcome to Chapter 23 of "Strike Deals Like a Pro: Unleash Your Inner Negotiation Ninja and Command Supplier Success." In this chapter, we'll explore the importance of cultivating long-term relationships with your suppliers and how to nurture these relationships for mutual benefit and success.

Here's what we'll cover in this chapter:

1. Understanding the value of long-term relationships: Delve into why long-term relationships with suppliers are essential for fostering trust, collaboration, and stability in your supply chain. Learn about the benefits of continuity, reliability, and shared success that come with cultivating long-term partnerships.
2. Building trust and rapport: Explore techniques for building trust and rapport with your suppliers, laying the foundation for a strong and enduring relationship. Learn how to communicate openly, demonstrate integrity, and deliver on your commitments to earn your supplier's trust and respect.
3. Communication and transparency: Discover the importance of communication and transparency in maintaining healthy supplier relationships. Learn how to keep your suppliers informed about changes, challenges, and opportunities in your business, and seek their input and

feedback to foster collaboration and alignment.
4. Collaboration and value creation: Explore strategies for collaborating with your suppliers to create value and drive innovation. Learn how to involve suppliers in product development, process improvement, and cost-saving initiatives, leveraging their expertise and insights to mutual benefit.
5. Managing conflicts and disagreements: Understand how to effectively manage conflicts and disagreements that may arise in long-term supplier relationships. Learn techniques for addressing concerns, resolving disputes, and maintaining open lines of communication to prevent issues from escalating.
6. Continuous improvement and feedback: Explore the importance of continuous improvement and feedback in nurturing long-term relationships with your suppliers. Learn how to solicit feedback from your suppliers, identify areas for

improvement, and implement changes to enhance collaboration and performance.

Throughout this chapter, we'll delve into real-world examples, case studies, and practical exercises to help you master the art of cultivating long-term relationships with your suppliers. By investing in trust, communication, collaboration, and continuous improvement, you'll strengthen your supplier relationships, enhance your supply chain resilience, and achieve sustainable success in your business endeavors. So, let's dive in and uncover the secrets to cultivating long-term relationships like a negotiation ninja!

Chapter 24: Managing Supplier Performance

Welcome to Chapter 24 of "Strike Deals Like a Pro: Unleash Your Inner Negotiation Ninja and Command Supplier Success." In this chapter, we'll explore the crucial aspect of managing supplier performance to ensure that your agreements are upheld, quality standards are met, and expectations are exceeded.

Here's what we'll cover in this chapter:

1. Setting clear performance metrics: Delve into the importance of setting clear performance metrics and key performance indicators (KPIs) to measure supplier performance effectively. Learn how to define specific, measurable, achievable, relevant, and time-bound metrics that align with your business objectives.
2. Monitoring supplier performance: Explore techniques for monitoring supplier performance against established metrics and KPIs. Learn how to collect relevant data, track progress, and identify trends or areas of concern that may require attention.
3. Providing constructive feedback: Discover the value of providing constructive feedback to your suppliers to help them understand expectations, address performance issues, and make continuous

improvements. Learn how to communicate feedback effectively, focusing on specific behaviors or outcomes rather than personal criticism.
4. Addressing performance issues: Understand how to address performance issues with your suppliers in a proactive and constructive manner. Learn techniques for identifying root causes, analyzing contributing factors, and developing action plans to address deficiencies and prevent recurrence.
5. Collaborative problem-solving: Explore strategies for collaboratively problem-solving with your suppliers to overcome performance challenges and drive improvement. Learn how to engage in open dialogue, explore alternative solutions, and work together to implement corrective actions.
6. Recognizing and rewarding success: Discover the importance of recognizing and rewarding your suppliers for outstanding performance and contributions to your business success. Learn how to celebrate achievements,

acknowledge exceptional efforts, and reinforce positive behaviors to motivate continued excellence.

Throughout this chapter, we'll delve into real-world examples, case studies, and practical exercises to help you master the art of managing supplier performance effectively. By setting clear expectations, monitoring performance, providing feedback, and collaborating on solutions, you'll enhance your supplier relationships, drive continuous improvement, and achieve better outcomes in your business endeavors. So, let's dive in and uncover the secrets to managing supplier performance like a negotiation ninja!

Chapter 25: Adapting to Changing Market Conditions

Welcome to Chapter 25 of "Strike Deals Like a Pro: Unleash Your Inner Negotiation Ninja and Command Supplier Success." In this chapter, we'll explore the importance of adapting to changing market conditions in supplier negotiations and strategies for navigating uncertainty effectively.

Here's what we'll cover in this chapter:

1. Understanding market dynamics: Delve into the factors that influence market dynamics, including supply and demand fluctuations, economic trends, regulatory changes, and technological advancements. Learn how these factors can impact negotiation strategies, pricing, and supplier relationships.
2. Monitoring market trends: Explore techniques for monitoring market trends and staying informed about changes that may affect your business or industry. Learn how to gather market intelligence, analyze data, and identify emerging opportunities or threats in your supply chain.
3. Agility and flexibility: Discover the value of agility and flexibility in adapting to changing market conditions. Learn how to adjust your negotiation approach, sourcing strategies, and supply chain operations in

response to shifting market dynamics and customer demands.

4. Scenario planning: Understand the importance of scenario planning in preparing for uncertain futures. Learn how to anticipate potential market scenarios, assess their impact on your business, and develop contingency plans to mitigate risks and capitalize on opportunities.
5. Collaborative innovation: Explore the role of collaborative innovation in responding to changing market conditions. Learn how to collaborate with your suppliers to co-create new products, services, or solutions that address evolving customer needs and market trends.
6. Continuous improvement: Discover the importance of continuous improvement in maintaining competitiveness and resilience in dynamic markets. Learn how to foster a culture of innovation, learning, and adaptation within your organization and supply chain ecosystem.

Throughout this chapter, we'll delve into real-world examples, case studies, and practical exercises to help you master the art of adapting to changing market conditions. By staying vigilant, agile, and proactive in response to market dynamics, you'll enhance your negotiation effectiveness, strengthen your supplier relationships, and achieve better outcomes in your business endeavors. So, let's dive in and uncover the secrets to adapting like a negotiation ninja!

Chapter 26: Leveraging Strategic Alliances

Welcome to Chapter 26 of "Strike Deals Like a Pro: Unleash Your Inner Negotiation Ninja and Command Supplier Success." In this chapter, we'll explore the power of strategic alliances in supplier negotiations and how they can help you achieve your business objectives more effectively.

Here's what we'll cover in this chapter:

1. Understanding strategic alliances: Delve into the concept of strategic alliances and their role in supplier negotiations. Learn how strategic alliances involve collaborative partnerships between businesses to achieve mutual goals, such as market expansion, innovation, or cost savings.
2. Types of strategic alliances: Explore different types of strategic alliances,

including joint ventures, partnerships, consortia, and alliances. Learn about the benefits and challenges associated with each type of alliance and how they can be leveraged in supplier negotiations.
3. Identifying potential partners: Discover strategies for identifying potential partners for strategic alliances in supplier negotiations. Learn how to assess compatibility, alignment of interests, and complementary strengths to identify partners that can help you achieve your negotiation objectives.
4. Negotiating alliance agreements: Explore techniques for negotiating alliance agreements with your partners, including terms of collaboration, resource sharing, decision-making processes, and dispute resolution mechanisms. Learn how to balance the interests of all parties involved and create win-win agreements that facilitate cooperation and value creation.
5. Managing alliance relationships: Understand the importance of managing alliance relationships effectively to ensure their success. Learn how to establish clear

communication channels, build trust, and resolve conflicts or disagreements that may arise in the course of the alliance.
6. Evaluating alliance performance: Discover how to evaluate the performance of your strategic alliances and measure their impact on your business objectives. Learn techniques for assessing key performance indicators, identifying areas for improvement, and making adjustments to optimize alliance outcomes.

Throughout this chapter, we'll delve into real-world examples, case studies, and practical exercises to help you master the art of leveraging strategic alliances in supplier negotiations. By forming strategic partnerships and alliances, you'll enhance your negotiation effectiveness, expand your capabilities, and achieve better outcomes in your business endeavors. So, let's dive in and uncover the secrets to leveraging strategic alliances like a negotiation ninja!

Chapter 27: Sustainable Sourcing Practices

Welcome to Chapter 27 of "Strike Deals Like a Pro: Unleash Your Inner Negotiation Ninja and Command Supplier Success." In this chapter, we'll explore the importance of sustainable sourcing practices in supplier negotiations and how they can contribute to long-term business success.

Here's what we'll cover in this chapter:

1. Understanding sustainability in sourcing: Delve into the concept of sustainability in sourcing and its significance for businesses, society, and the environment. Learn how sustainable sourcing practices aim to minimize negative impacts on the planet, promote social responsibility, and ensure ethical supply chains.
2. Key principles of sustainable sourcing: Explore the key principles of sustainable sourcing, including environmental stewardship, social equity, economic

viability, and transparency. Learn how these principles guide decision-making in supplier negotiations and procurement processes.
3. Sustainable sourcing strategies: Discover strategies for integrating sustainability into your sourcing practices and supplier negotiations. Learn how to assess supplier sustainability performance, prioritize sustainable criteria in supplier selection, and incentivize suppliers to adopt sustainable practices.
4. Collaborative sustainability initiatives: Explore the role of collaborative sustainability initiatives in supplier negotiations. Learn how businesses can work together with suppliers, industry peers, and stakeholders to address sustainability challenges, share best practices, and drive collective action for positive change.
5. Metrics and measurement: Understand the importance of metrics and measurement in tracking progress towards sustainability goals. Learn how to define key

performance indicators (KPIs), collect relevant data, and evaluate supplier performance against sustainability criteria.
6. Continuous improvement and innovation: Discover how to foster continuous improvement and innovation in sustainable sourcing practices. Learn techniques for encouraging suppliers to innovate and adopt new technologies, materials, or processes that reduce environmental impact and improve social outcomes.

Throughout this chapter, we'll delve into real-world examples, case studies, and practical exercises to help you master the art of sustainable sourcing in supplier negotiations. By integrating sustainability principles into your sourcing strategies, you'll enhance your brand reputation, mitigate risks, and contribute to a more sustainable future for your business and the planet. So, let's dive in and uncover the secrets to sustainable sourcing like a negotiation ninja!

Chapter 28: Ethical Considerations in Supplier Negotiations

Welcome to Chapter 28 of "Strike Deals Like a Pro: Unleash Your Inner Negotiation Ninja and Command Supplier Success." In this chapter, we'll explore the ethical considerations that arise in supplier negotiations and how to navigate them with integrity and professionalism.

Here's what we'll cover in this chapter:

1. Understanding ethical dilemmas: Delve into common ethical dilemmas that may arise in supplier negotiations, such as conflicts of interest, bribery, corruption, and exploitation of workers or natural resources. Learn how these dilemmas can

impact business relationships, reputation, and long-term sustainability.
2. Ethical decision-making frameworks: Explore frameworks for ethical decision-making in supplier negotiations, such as utilitarianism, deontology, virtue ethics, and stakeholder theory. Learn how to evaluate the ethical implications of different courses of action and make decisions that prioritize ethical considerations.
3. Transparency and honesty: Discover the importance of transparency and honesty in supplier negotiations. Learn how to communicate openly with your suppliers, disclose relevant information, and avoid misleading or deceptive practices that undermine trust and integrity.
4. Fair treatment of suppliers: Explore strategies for ensuring fair treatment of suppliers throughout the negotiation process. Learn how to negotiate in good faith, respect supplier rights, and uphold contractual agreements to promote fairness and equity in business relationships.

5. Compliance with laws and regulations: Understand the importance of compliance with laws and regulations governing supplier negotiations, such as anti-corruption laws, labor standards, and environmental regulations. Learn how to ensure that your negotiation practices align with legal requirements and ethical standards.
6. Corporate social responsibility (CSR): Discover the role of corporate social responsibility (CSR) in supplier negotiations and procurement processes. Learn how to integrate CSR principles into your business practices, including supplier selection criteria, performance evaluations, and sustainability initiatives.

Throughout this chapter, we'll delve into real-world examples, case studies, and practical exercises to help you navigate ethical considerations in supplier negotiations. By upholding ethical standards and promoting integrity in your negotiation practices, you'll enhance your reputation, build trust with your suppliers, and contribute to a more ethical and sustainable business environment. So, let's dive in and uncover the secrets to ethical negotiation like a negotiation ninja!

Chapter 29: Managing Cultural Differences in Supplier Negotiations

Welcome to Chapter 29 of "Strike Deals Like a Pro: Unleash Your Inner Negotiation Ninja and Command Supplier Success." In this chapter, we'll explore the challenges and opportunities of managing cultural differences in supplier negotiations and how to navigate them effectively.

Here's what we'll cover in this chapter:

1. Understanding cultural diversity: Delve into the concept of cultural diversity and its impact on supplier negotiations. Learn how cultural differences in communication styles, attitudes toward time, hierarchy, and

decision-making processes can influence negotiation dynamics.
2. Cultural intelligence: Explore the importance of cultural intelligence (CQ) in navigating cultural differences effectively. Learn how to develop your cultural awareness, sensitivity, and adaptability to communicate and negotiate successfully with individuals from diverse cultural backgrounds.
3. Cross-cultural communication: Discover strategies for effective cross-cultural communication in supplier negotiations. Learn how to overcome language barriers, clarify meanings, and interpret non-verbal cues to ensure mutual understanding and trust.
4. Building rapport and trust: Understand the role of building rapport and trust in bridging cultural differences and establishing productive relationships with your suppliers. Learn techniques for demonstrating respect, empathy, and openness to foster goodwill and collaboration.

5. Negotiation styles and strategies: Explore how negotiation styles and strategies vary across cultures and how to adjust your approach accordingly. Learn how to adapt to different preferences for direct vs. indirect communication, competitive vs. collaborative negotiation, and relationship-building vs. task-focused interactions.
6. Resolving cultural conflicts: Discover techniques for resolving cultural conflicts and misunderstandings that may arise in supplier negotiations. Learn how to address differences in values, norms, and expectations through open dialogue, compromise, and mutual respect.

Throughout this chapter, we'll delve into real-world examples, case studies, and practical exercises to help you master the art of managing cultural differences in supplier negotiations. By embracing cultural diversity, building cultural intelligence, and adapting your negotiation approach to different cultural contexts, you'll enhance your negotiation effectiveness, strengthen your supplier relationships, and achieve better outcomes in your business endeavors. So, let's dive in and uncover the secrets to managing cultural differences like a negotiation ninja!

Chapter 30: Crisis Management in Supplier Relationships

Welcome to Chapter 30 of "Strike Deals Like a Pro: Unleash Your Inner Negotiation Ninja and Command Supplier Success." In this chapter, we'll explore the challenges of crisis management in supplier relationships and strategies for effectively navigating crises to preserve business continuity and mitigate risk.

Here's what we'll cover in this chapter:

1. Understanding supplier relationship crises: Delve into the various types of crises that can arise in supplier relationships, such as supply chain disruptions, quality issues, financial instability, or reputational

damage. Learn how these crises can impact your business operations and bottom line.
2. Crisis preparedness: Explore the importance of crisis preparedness in mitigating the impact of supplier relationship crises. Learn how to develop contingency plans, assess risk exposure, and establish communication protocols to respond swiftly and effectively to crises as they arise.
3. Communication and transparency: Discover the role of communication and transparency in crisis management. Learn how to communicate openly with your suppliers, stakeholders, and customers during times of crisis, providing timely updates, sharing relevant information, and addressing concerns to maintain trust and confidence.
4. Collaborative problem-solving: Explore strategies for collaborative problem-solving in crisis situations. Learn how to work together with your suppliers to identify root causes, assess the impact of the crisis, and develop solutions that

minimize disruption and restore business operations as quickly as possible.
5. Risk mitigation and contingency planning: Understand how to mitigate risks and develop contingency plans to prepare for potential supplier relationship crises. Learn techniques for diversifying your supplier base, securing alternative sources of supply, and implementing robust risk management strategies to enhance resilience.
6. Learning from crises: Discover the value of learning from crises to strengthen your supplier relationships and improve crisis preparedness in the future. Learn how to conduct post-crisis evaluations, identify lessons learned, and implement changes to prevent similar crises from occurring again.

Throughout this chapter, we'll delve into real-world examples, case studies, and practical exercises to help you master the art of crisis management in supplier relationships. By adopting proactive crisis preparedness measures, maintaining open communication, and collaborating effectively with your suppliers, you'll enhance your ability to navigate crises successfully and preserve business continuity in the face of adversity. So, let's dive in and uncover the secrets to crisis management like a negotiation ninja!

Chapter 31: Leveraging Technology in Supplier Negotiations

Welcome to Chapter 31 of "Strike Deals Like a Pro: Unleash Your Inner Negotiation Ninja and Command Supplier Success." In this chapter, we'll explore the role of technology in modern supplier negotiations and how you can leverage it to streamline processes, enhance communication, and drive better outcomes.

Here's what we'll cover in this chapter:

1. The digital transformation of supplier negotiations: Delve into the digital transformation of supplier negotiations and the emergence of technology-driven

solutions to improve efficiency, transparency, and collaboration in the negotiation process.
2. Digital negotiation platforms: Explore the features and benefits of digital negotiation platforms, such as e-sourcing tools, online bidding platforms, and contract management systems. Learn how these platforms can help you automate repetitive tasks, centralize negotiation data, and standardize processes to save time and resources.
3. Data analytics and predictive modeling: Discover how data analytics and predictive modeling can provide valuable insights into supplier performance, market trends, and negotiation outcomes. Learn how to leverage data-driven insights to make more informed decisions, optimize negotiation strategies, and identify opportunities for cost savings or risk mitigation.
4. Collaboration tools and virtual communication: Explore the role of collaboration tools and virtual communication platforms in facilitating remote negotiations and cross-border collaboration. Learn how to use video conferencing, instant messaging, and document sharing tools to communicate effectively with your suppliers and

stakeholders, regardless of geographic location.
5. Blockchain and smart contracts: Understand how blockchain technology and smart contracts can enhance transparency, security, and trust in supplier negotiations. Learn how blockchain can be used to track and verify transactions, authenticate product origins, and enforce contract terms automatically, reducing the risk of disputes or fraud.
6. Artificial intelligence and machine learning: Delve into the potential applications of artificial intelligence (AI) and machine learning in supplier negotiations, such as natural language processing, sentiment analysis, and predictive modeling. Learn how AI-powered tools can augment decision-making, automate routine tasks, and optimize negotiation outcomes based on historical data and real-time insights.

Throughout this chapter, we'll delve into real-world examples, case studies, and practical tips to help you harness the power of technology in supplier negotiations. By embracing digital tools and innovative technologies, you'll enhance your negotiation effectiveness, improve collaboration with your suppliers, and achieve better outcomes in your business endeavors. So, let's dive in and uncover the secrets to leveraging technology like a negotiation ninja!

Chapter 32: Negotiating Sustainable Pricing Models

Welcome to Chapter 32 of "Strike Deals Like a Pro: Unleash Your Inner Negotiation Ninja and Command Supplier Success." In this chapter, we'll explore the concept of negotiating sustainable pricing models in supplier negotiations and how to create agreements that benefit both parties in the long term.

Here's what we'll cover in this chapter:

1. Understanding sustainable pricing: Delve into the importance of sustainable pricing in supplier negotiations, which involves establishing fair and equitable pricing structures that consider the needs and interests of both buyers and suppliers.

2. Total cost of ownership (TCO) analysis: Explore the concept of total cost of ownership (TCO) analysis and its role in negotiating sustainable pricing models. Learn how to assess the total costs associated with procuring goods or services, including acquisition costs, operating costs, and lifecycle costs, to inform pricing decisions.
3. Value-based pricing: Discover the principles of value-based pricing and how it can be applied in supplier negotiations. Learn how to align pricing with the perceived value of goods or services, taking into account factors such as quality, innovation, and customer benefits, to create win-win agreements that maximize value for both parties.
4. Long-term partnership pricing: Explore the benefits of adopting a long-term partnership approach to pricing in supplier negotiations. Learn how to negotiate pricing agreements that reflect the value of ongoing collaboration, innovation, and shared risk mitigation strategies, fostering

trust and loyalty between buyers and suppliers.
5. Risk-sharing pricing models: Understand the concept of risk-sharing pricing models and how they can be used to create mutually beneficial agreements in supplier negotiations. Learn how to allocate risks and rewards between buyers and suppliers based on their respective capabilities, contributions, and exposure to risk factors.
6. Performance-based pricing incentives: Delve into the use of performance-based pricing incentives to incentivize desired supplier behaviors and outcomes. Learn how to structure pricing agreements that tie payments to key performance indicators (KPIs), quality metrics, or achievement of shared goals, encouraging suppliers to deliver value and continuous improvement.

Throughout this chapter, we'll delve into real-world examples, case studies, and practical exercises to help you master the art of negotiating sustainable pricing models in supplier negotiations. By adopting a strategic approach to pricing that considers the long-term interests of both parties, you'll enhance your negotiation effectiveness, build stronger relationships with your suppliers, and achieve better outcomes in your business endeavors. So, let's dive in and uncover the secrets to negotiating sustainable pricing like a negotiation ninja!

Chapter 33: Leveraging Negotiation Power Dynamics

Welcome to Chapter 33 of "Strike Deals Like a Pro: Unleash Your Inner Negotiation Ninja and Command Supplier Success." In this chapter, we'll explore the dynamics of negotiation power and how to leverage them effectively to achieve your objectives in supplier negotiations.

Here's what we'll cover in this chapter:

1. Understanding negotiation power: Delve into the concept of negotiation power and

its various sources, including information, alternatives, resources, and relationships. Learn how power dynamics influence negotiation outcomes and strategies.
2. Assessing power dynamics: Explore techniques for assessing power dynamics in supplier negotiations, including analyzing relative strengths and weaknesses, identifying sources of leverage, and understanding the balance of power between parties.
3. Building negotiation power: Discover strategies for building negotiation power and enhancing your leverage in supplier negotiations. Learn how to strengthen your position through preparation, information gathering, relationship building, and alternative development.
4. Exploiting power differentials: Understand how to exploit power differentials to your advantage in supplier negotiations. Learn techniques for leveraging your strengths, mitigating your weaknesses, and capitalizing on opportunities to influence the negotiation process and outcomes.

5. **Balancing power:** Explore the importance of balancing power in supplier negotiations to maintain fairness, trust, and long-term relationships. Learn how to avoid excessive use of power tactics that may damage relationships or lead to suboptimal outcomes for both parties.
6. **Negotiating win-win solutions:** Delve into strategies for negotiating win-win solutions that satisfy the interests of both parties while leveraging negotiation power effectively. Learn how to create value, expand the negotiation pie, and foster collaboration to achieve mutually beneficial outcomes.

Throughout this chapter, we'll delve into real-world examples, case studies, and practical exercises to help you master the art of leveraging negotiation power dynamics in supplier negotiations. By understanding and effectively managing negotiation power, you'll enhance your negotiation effectiveness, build stronger relationships with your suppliers, and achieve better outcomes in your business endeavors. So, let's dive in and uncover the secrets to leveraging negotiation power like a negotiation ninja!

Chapter 34: Overcoming Common Negotiation Challenges

Welcome to Chapter 34 of "Strike Deals Like a Pro: Unleash Your Inner Negotiation Ninja and Command Supplier Success." In this chapter, we'll explore common challenges that arise in supplier negotiations and strategies for overcoming them effectively.

Here's what we'll cover in this chapter:

1. Identifying common negotiation challenges: Delve into common challenges that negotiators face in supplier negotiations, such as communication barriers, conflict resolution, power imbalances, and resistance to change. Learn how these challenges can impact negotiation outcomes and relationships with suppliers.
2. Effective communication strategies: Explore techniques for overcoming communication barriers and fostering open, constructive dialogue in supplier negotiations. Learn how to listen actively, ask probing questions, and clarify misunderstandings to ensure mutual understanding and alignment.
3. Managing conflict and resistance: Discover strategies for managing conflict and overcoming resistance in supplier negotiations. Learn how to address differences of opinion, negotiate win-win solutions, and build consensus among

stakeholders to move negotiations forward.
4. Navigating power dynamics: Understand how to navigate power dynamics and address imbalances effectively in supplier negotiations. Learn techniques for leveraging your strengths, mitigating weaknesses, and building alliances to enhance your negotiating position.
5. Adapting to cultural differences: Explore how to adapt to cultural differences and bridge cultural divides in supplier negotiations. Learn how to recognize and respect cultural norms, preferences, and communication styles to build rapport and trust with your counterparts.
6. Problem-solving and creativity: Delve into problem-solving techniques and creative thinking strategies to overcome negotiation challenges. Learn how to brainstorm innovative solutions, explore alternative options, and think outside the box to break through impasses and find mutually acceptable agreements.

Throughout this chapter, we'll delve into real-world examples, case studies, and practical exercises to help you overcome common negotiation challenges in supplier negotiations. By equipping yourself with effective communication skills, conflict resolution techniques, and problem-solving strategies, you'll enhance your negotiation effectiveness, build stronger relationships with your suppliers, and achieve better outcomes in your business endeavors. So, let's dive in and uncover the secrets to overcoming negotiation challenges like a negotiation ninja!

Chapter 35: Mastering Contract Negotiation

Welcome to Chapter 35 of "Strike Deals Like a Pro: Unleash Your Inner Negotiation Ninja and Command Supplier Success." In this chapter, we'll explore the intricacies of contract negotiation in supplier relationships and how to master this critical aspect of the negotiation process.

Here's what we'll cover in this chapter:

1. Understanding the importance of contracts: Delve into the importance of contracts in supplier relationships and how they serve as the foundation for defining rights, responsibilities, and expectations between parties. Learn how well-crafted contracts can mitigate risks, clarify terms, and prevent disputes.
2. Key elements of a contract: Explore the key elements of a contract and how they should be negotiated to protect your interests and achieve your objectives. Learn about essential clauses, such as scope of work, pricing, delivery terms, quality standards, warranties, and dispute resolution mechanisms.
3. Negotiating contract terms: Discover strategies for negotiating contract terms that align with your business objectives and mitigate risks. Learn how to prioritize

negotiation points, anticipate potential issues, and advocate for favorable terms while maintaining a collaborative and constructive negotiation environment.
4. Balancing flexibility and certainty: Understand the importance of balancing flexibility and certainty in contract negotiation. Learn how to strike the right balance between clear, enforceable terms and provisions that allow for adaptation to changing circumstances or unforeseen events.
5. Assessing legal and commercial risks: Explore techniques for assessing legal and commercial risks in contract negotiation and mitigating them effectively. Learn how to conduct risk assessments, identify potential liabilities, and negotiate risk allocation provisions to protect your interests and minimize exposure.
6. Finalizing and executing contracts: Delve into best practices for finalizing and executing contracts once negotiation is complete. Learn about the importance of thorough review, documentation, and approval processes to ensure that

contracts accurately reflect negotiated terms and are legally binding.

Throughout this chapter, we'll delve into real-world examples, case studies, and practical exercises to help you master the art of contract negotiation in supplier relationships. By developing your negotiation skills and understanding the nuances of contract negotiation, you'll enhance your ability to create fair, enforceable agreements that support your business objectives and strengthen your relationships with suppliers. So, let's dive in and uncover the secrets to mastering contract negotiation like a negotiation ninja!

Chapter 36: Managing Supplier Relationships

Welcome to Chapter 36 of "Strike Deals Like a Pro: Unleash Your Inner Negotiation Ninja and Command Supplier Success." In this chapter, we'll explore the importance of effectively managing supplier relationships beyond the negotiation process and how to cultivate partnerships that drive mutual success.

Here's what we'll cover in this chapter:

1. The importance of supplier relationships: Delve into why supplier relationships are crucial for business success, including factors such as reliability, quality, innovation, and cost-effectiveness. Learn how strong supplier relationships contribute to competitive advantage, risk mitigation, and long-term sustainability.
2. Building trust and rapport: Explore strategies for building trust and rapport with your suppliers to foster open communication, collaboration, and mutual respect. Learn how to demonstrate reliability, integrity, and transparency in your interactions to build strong, enduring partnerships.
3. Effective communication strategies: Discover techniques for effective communication with your suppliers to ensure clarity, alignment, and

understanding. Learn how to establish regular communication channels, provide timely feedback, and address issues promptly to maintain positive relationships.
4. Collaboration and co-creation: Understand the value of collaboration and co-creation with your suppliers to drive innovation, efficiency, and value creation. Learn how to involve suppliers in product development, process improvement, and problem-solving to leverage their expertise and insights.
5. Performance monitoring and feedback: Explore methods for monitoring supplier performance and providing constructive feedback to drive continuous improvement. Learn how to establish performance metrics, conduct regular evaluations, and communicate feedback in a supportive, constructive manner.
6. Resolving conflicts and addressing issues: Delve into strategies for resolving conflicts and addressing issues that may arise in supplier relationships. Learn how to

approach difficult conversations, find common ground, and work together with your suppliers to find mutually acceptable solutions.

Throughout this chapter, we'll delve into real-world examples, case studies, and practical exercises to help you master the art of managing supplier relationships. By nurturing strong, collaborative partnerships with your suppliers, you'll enhance your organization's competitiveness, resilience, and ability to adapt to changing market conditions. So, let's dive in and uncover the secrets to managing supplier relationships like a negotiation ninja!

Chapter 37: Supplier Performance Management

Welcome to Chapter 37 of "Strike Deals Like a Pro: Unleash Your Inner Negotiation Ninja and Command Supplier Success." In this chapter, we'll explore the critical aspect of supplier performance management and how it contributes to the success of your business.

Here's what we'll cover in this chapter:

1. Importance of supplier performance management: Delve into why supplier performance management is essential for ensuring the quality, reliability, and consistency of goods and services provided by suppliers. Learn how effective performance management contributes to cost savings, risk mitigation, and customer satisfaction.
2. Key performance indicators (KPIs): Explore the key performance indicators (KPIs) used to measure supplier performance across various dimensions, such as quality, delivery, cost, responsiveness, and innovation. Learn how to define relevant KPIs that align with your business objectives and supplier expectations.
3. Performance measurement and evaluation: Discover techniques for measuring and evaluating supplier performance against

established KPIs. Learn how to collect performance data, analyze performance metrics, and assess supplier capabilities to identify areas for improvement and recognize exceptional performance.
4. Performance feedback and communication: Understand the importance of providing timely, constructive feedback to your suppliers to drive continuous improvement. Learn how to communicate performance expectations, share performance data, and collaborate with suppliers to address performance issues and implement corrective actions.
5. Performance improvement strategies: Explore strategies for collaborating with suppliers to improve performance and achieve mutually beneficial outcomes. Learn how to identify root causes of performance issues, develop action plans for improvement, and monitor progress to ensure sustainable results.
6. Supplier recognition and rewards: Delve into the role of supplier recognition and rewards in motivating and incentivizing

high performance. Learn how to acknowledge and celebrate suppliers that consistently meet or exceed performance expectations, fostering a culture of excellence and partnership.

Throughout this chapter, we'll delve into real-world examples, case studies, and practical exercises to help you master the art of supplier performance management. By implementing effective performance management practices, you'll enhance the reliability, efficiency, and competitiveness of your supply chain, driving business success and customer satisfaction. So, let's dive in and uncover the secrets to supplier performance management like a negotiation ninja!

Chapter 38: Supply Chain Risk Management

Welcome to Chapter 38 of "Strike Deals Like a Pro: Unleash Your Inner Negotiation Ninja and

Command Supplier Success." In this chapter, we'll explore the critical topic of supply chain risk management and how to mitigate risks effectively to ensure business continuity and resilience.

Here's what we'll cover in this chapter:

1. Understanding supply chain risks: Delve into the various types of risks that can affect supply chains, including natural disasters, geopolitical instability, economic downturns, supplier failures, and cybersecurity threats. Learn how these risks can impact your business operations and bottom line.
2. Risk assessment and identification: Explore techniques for assessing and identifying supply chain risks to understand their potential impact and likelihood of occurrence. Learn how to conduct risk assessments, map supply chain dependencies, and prioritize risks based on their severity and probability.
3. Risk mitigation strategies: Discover strategies for mitigating supply chain risks

to minimize their impact on your business. Learn about preventive measures, such as diversifying your supplier base, implementing redundancy or backup plans, and securing insurance coverage to protect against unforeseen events.

4. Supplier risk management: Understand the importance of supplier risk management in mitigating risks throughout the supply chain. Learn how to evaluate supplier risk factors, such as financial stability, operational resilience, and compliance with regulations, to assess their risk exposure and implement risk mitigation measures.

5. Continuity planning and resilience: Explore the concept of continuity planning and resilience in supply chain risk management. Learn how to develop contingency plans, business continuity plans, and crisis management protocols to respond effectively to supply chain disruptions and ensure business continuity.

6. Monitoring and adaptation: Delve into the importance of monitoring supply chain risks and adapting your risk management

strategies as circumstances change. Learn how to establish early warning systems, track key risk indicators, and implement agile risk management practices to respond proactively to emerging threats.

Throughout this chapter, we'll delve into real-world examples, case studies, and practical exercises to help you master the art of supply chain risk management. By identifying, assessing, and mitigating supply chain risks effectively, you'll enhance the resilience, agility, and competitiveness of your business, enabling you to thrive in an increasingly volatile and uncertain business environment. So, let's dive in and uncover the secrets to supply chain risk management like a negotiation ninja!

Chapter 39: Sustainable Procurement Practices

Welcome to Chapter 39 of "Strike Deals Like a Pro: Unleash Your Inner Negotiation Ninja and Command Supplier Success." In this chapter, we'll explore the principles and practices of sustainable procurement and how they contribute to environmental stewardship, social responsibility, and long-term business success.

Here's what we'll cover in this chapter:

1. Introduction to sustainable procurement: Delve into the concept of sustainable procurement and its importance for organizations seeking to minimize their environmental footprint, promote social equity, and drive positive change throughout their supply chains.
2. Sustainable procurement principles: Explore the key principles of sustainable procurement, including environmental sustainability, social responsibility, ethical sourcing, and economic viability. Learn how these principles guide decision-making and procurement practices to achieve sustainability goals.
3. Sustainable sourcing strategies: Discover strategies for integrating sustainability into your procurement processes and supplier relationships. Learn how to assess supplier

sustainability performance, prioritize sustainable criteria in supplier selection, and collaborate with suppliers to drive continuous improvement.
4. Green procurement initiatives: Understand the role of green procurement initiatives in promoting environmental sustainability and reducing carbon emissions. Learn how to prioritize environmentally friendly products and services, minimize waste and pollution, and support suppliers that demonstrate a commitment to sustainability.
5. Socially responsible procurement: Explore strategies for promoting social responsibility and ethical sourcing in procurement practices. Learn how to ensure fair labor practices, respect human rights, and support diversity and inclusion initiatives throughout your supply chain.
6. Sustainable procurement metrics and reporting: Delve into the importance of metrics and reporting in measuring and communicating the impact of sustainable procurement practices. Learn how to define key performance indicators (KPIs),

collect relevant data, and report on sustainability performance to stakeholders.

Throughout this chapter, we'll delve into real-world examples, case studies, and practical exercises to help you master the art of sustainable procurement. By adopting sustainable procurement practices, you'll enhance your organization's reputation, reduce risk exposure, and create value for your business, society, and the environment. So, let's dive in and uncover the secrets to sustainable procurement like a negotiation ninja!

Chapter 40: Supplier Diversity and Inclusion Initiatives

Welcome to Chapter 40 of "Strike Deals Like a Pro: Unleash Your Inner Negotiation Ninja and Command Supplier Success." In this chapter, we'll explore the importance of supplier diversity and inclusion initiatives and how they contribute to business success and societal impact.

Here's what we'll cover in this chapter:

1. Introduction to supplier diversity and inclusion: Delve into the concept of supplier diversity and inclusion and why it's essential for organizations to embrace diversity in their supply chains. Learn how supplier diversity initiatives support economic empowerment, innovation, and social equity.
2. Benefits of supplier diversity: Explore the benefits of supplier diversity for both buyers and suppliers, including increased competition, access to new markets, innovation, and improved corporate reputation. Learn how supplier diversity initiatives contribute to economic development and job creation in diverse communities.
3. Implementing supplier diversity programs: Discover strategies for implementing

supplier diversity programs within your organization, including setting goals, establishing policies and procedures, and creating support structures to ensure program success. Learn how to engage stakeholders, promote awareness, and foster a culture of inclusion.

4. Supplier diversity metrics and measurement: Understand the importance of measuring and tracking supplier diversity performance using key performance indicators (KPIs) and metrics. Learn how to assess the effectiveness of your supplier diversity initiatives, identify areas for improvement, and report on progress to stakeholders.

5. Supplier diversity best practices: Explore best practices for promoting supplier diversity and inclusion throughout the procurement process. Learn how to identify diverse suppliers, assess their capabilities, and provide support and resources to help them succeed. Discover strategies for building relationships and

fostering partnerships with diverse suppliers.
6. **Overcoming challenges and barriers:** Delve into common challenges and barriers to supplier diversity and inclusion and how to overcome them. Learn about potential obstacles, such as limited supplier capacity, unconscious bias, and resistance to change, and strategies for addressing them to maximize the impact of your supplier diversity initiatives.

Throughout this chapter, we'll delve into real-world examples, case studies, and practical exercises to help you master the art of supplier diversity and inclusion. By embracing supplier diversity initiatives, you'll not only drive business success and innovation but also contribute to a more inclusive and equitable society. So, let's dive in and uncover the secrets to supplier diversity and inclusion like a negotiation ninja!

Chapter 41: Ethical Sourcing and Corporate Social Responsibility

Welcome to Chapter 41 of "Strike Deals Like a Pro: Unleash Your Inner Negotiation Ninja and Command Supplier Success." In this chapter, we'll explore the importance of ethical sourcing and corporate social responsibility (CSR) in supplier relationships and how they contribute to sustainable business practices and positive social impact.

Here's what we'll cover in this chapter:

1. Introduction to ethical sourcing and CSR: Delve into the concepts of ethical sourcing and CSR and their significance for organizations committed to conducting business in an ethical, socially responsible manner. Learn how ethical sourcing practices and CSR initiatives support environmental stewardship, social welfare, and ethical business conduct.

2. Ethical considerations in supplier relationships: Explore the ethical considerations that organizations should take into account when engaging with suppliers, including labor practices, human rights, environmental impact, and business ethics. Learn how to assess supplier ethics and integrate ethical criteria into supplier selection and evaluation processes.
3. CSR in procurement practices: Discover how organizations can integrate CSR principles into their procurement practices to promote sustainability, diversity, and social inclusion throughout the supply chain. Learn how to prioritize suppliers that demonstrate a commitment to CSR, support local communities, and adhere to ethical standards.
4. Ethical audits and compliance: Understand the role of ethical audits and compliance in ensuring ethical sourcing practices and CSR standards are met throughout the supply chain. Learn how to conduct ethical audits, assess supplier compliance with ethical standards, and address non-compliance effectively through corrective actions and continuous monitoring.
5. Transparency and accountability: Explore the importance of transparency and

accountability in ethical sourcing and CSR initiatives. Learn how to communicate your organization's commitment to ethical sourcing practices, engage stakeholders in CSR efforts, and report on CSR performance to demonstrate accountability and build trust with customers, investors, and other stakeholders.
6. Supplier engagement and collaboration: Delve into strategies for engaging and collaborating with suppliers to promote ethical sourcing and CSR objectives. Learn how to build partnerships with suppliers based on shared values, mutual respect, and a commitment to sustainability, diversity, and social responsibility.

Throughout this chapter, we'll delve into real-world examples, case studies, and practical exercises to help you master the art of ethical sourcing and CSR in supplier relationships. By integrating ethical considerations and CSR principles into your procurement practices, you'll enhance your organization's reputation, mitigate risk, and create positive social impact. So, let's dive in and uncover the secrets to ethical sourcing and corporate social responsibility like a negotiation ninja!

Chapter 42: Conflict Resolution Strategies in Supplier Relationships

Welcome to Chapter 42 of "Strike Deals Like a Pro: Unleash Your Inner Negotiation Ninja and Command Supplier Success." In this chapter, we'll explore effective conflict resolution strategies to manage disputes and challenges that may arise in supplier relationships.

Here's what we'll cover in this chapter:

1. Understanding conflict in supplier relationships: Delve into the nature and causes of conflict in supplier relationships, including differences in goals, expectations, communication breakdowns, and resource constraints. Learn how unresolved conflicts can impact business operations and relationships with suppliers.
2. Conflict resolution approaches: Explore different approaches to conflict resolution, including negotiation, mediation,

arbitration, and litigation. Learn about the advantages and disadvantages of each approach and when to use them based on the nature and severity of the conflict.
3. Collaborative problem-solving: Discover the benefits of collaborative problem-solving in resolving conflicts and building stronger relationships with suppliers. Learn how to engage in constructive dialogue, identify underlying issues, and work together with suppliers to find mutually acceptable solutions.
4. Effective communication strategies: Understand the importance of effective communication in resolving conflicts in supplier relationships. Learn how to communicate openly, listen actively, and express concerns or grievances in a respectful, non-confrontational manner to facilitate resolution.
5. Conflict escalation and de-escalation: Explore techniques for de-escalating conflicts and preventing them from escalating into more significant issues. Learn how to recognize early warning signs

of conflict, address issues promptly, and de-escalate tensions through empathy, active listening, and compromise.
6. Establishing conflict resolution protocols: Delve into the importance of establishing conflict resolution protocols and procedures within your organization to address disputes in supplier relationships systematically. Learn how to develop clear escalation paths, define roles and responsibilities, and provide training and support to employees involved in conflict resolution.

Throughout this chapter, we'll delve into real-world examples, case studies, and practical exercises to help you master the art of conflict resolution in supplier relationships. By adopting effective conflict resolution strategies and fostering a culture of collaboration and communication, you'll enhance your ability to manage disputes and strengthen relationships with your suppliers. So, let's dive in and uncover the secrets to conflict resolution like a negotiation ninja!

Chapter 43: Supplier Performance Improvement Plans

Welcome to Chapter 43 of "Strike Deals Like a Pro: Unleash Your Inner Negotiation Ninja and Command Supplier Success." In this chapter, we'll explore the development and implementation of supplier performance improvement plans to address underperformance and drive continuous improvement in supplier relationships.

Here's what we'll cover in this chapter:

1. Identifying performance gaps: Delve into techniques for identifying performance gaps and areas for improvement in supplier relationships. Learn how to analyze performance data, conduct root cause analysis, and identify opportunities for enhancement to set the stage for improvement.

2. Establishing performance improvement goals: Explore the process of setting performance improvement goals and objectives that are specific, measurable, achievable, relevant, and time-bound (SMART). Learn how to align improvement goals with business objectives and supplier capabilities to drive meaningful progress.
3. Developing improvement strategies: Discover strategies for developing improvement strategies and action plans to address identified performance gaps. Learn how to prioritize improvement initiatives, allocate resources effectively, and engage stakeholders to support implementation efforts.
4. Collaboration and communication: Understand the importance of collaboration and communication in implementing performance improvement plans with suppliers. Learn how to engage suppliers in the improvement process, communicate expectations clearly, and establish feedback mechanisms to monitor progress.

5. Monitoring and measuring progress: Explore techniques for monitoring and measuring progress towards performance improvement goals. Learn how to track key performance indicators (KPIs), conduct regular performance reviews, and adjust improvement strategies as needed to stay on track.
6. Continuous improvement culture: Delve into the importance of fostering a culture of continuous improvement in supplier relationships. Learn how to celebrate successes, learn from failures, and encourage innovation and creativity to drive ongoing performance enhancement.

Throughout this chapter, we'll delve into real-world examples, case studies, and practical exercises to help you develop and implement supplier performance improvement plans effectively. By proactively addressing performance gaps and driving continuous improvement in supplier relationships, you'll enhance the reliability, quality, and value of goods and services provided by your suppliers, ultimately driving business success. So, let's dive in and uncover the secrets to supplier performance improvement like a negotiation ninja!

Chapter 44: Leveraging Technology for Supplier Relationship Management

Welcome to Chapter 44 of "Strike Deals Like a Pro: Unleash Your Inner Negotiation Ninja and Command Supplier Success." In this chapter, we'll explore how organizations can leverage technology to enhance supplier relationship management (SRM) practices and drive better outcomes in supplier relationships.

Here's what we'll cover in this chapter:

1. Introduction to technology-enabled SRM: Delve into the benefits of leveraging technology for SRM, including improved efficiency, visibility, collaboration, and decision-making. Learn how technology solutions can streamline SRM processes and enable organizations to extract more value from their supplier relationships.

2. SRM software and platforms: Explore the features and functionalities of SRM software and platforms designed to support supplier relationship management activities. Learn about key capabilities such as supplier performance tracking, contract management, risk assessment, and collaboration tools.
3. Data-driven insights: Understand how technology enables organizations to gather, analyze, and act upon data to gain insights into supplier performance, trends, and opportunities. Learn how to leverage data analytics, dashboards, and reporting tools to make informed decisions and drive continuous improvement in supplier relationships.
4. Automation and digitization: Discover how automation and digitization can streamline SRM processes and reduce manual effort. Learn how to automate routine tasks such as supplier onboarding, performance evaluations, and contract renewals to free up time for strategic activities.

5. Collaboration and communication tools: Explore technology-enabled collaboration and communication tools that facilitate engagement and interaction with suppliers. Learn how to use online portals, messaging platforms, and virtual meeting tools to communicate effectively, share information, and collaborate with suppliers in real time.
6. Integration with other systems: Delve into the importance of integrating SRM technology with other enterprise systems, such as ERP, CRM, and supply chain management systems. Learn how integration enables seamless data flow, process alignment, and decision-making across the organization.

Throughout this chapter, we'll delve into real-world examples, case studies, and practical insights to help you harness the power of technology for supplier relationship management. By embracing technology solutions tailored to SRM, you'll enhance your organization's ability to collaborate with suppliers, drive performance improvement, and achieve better outcomes in your supplier relationships. So, let's dive in and uncover the secrets to leveraging technology for SRM like a negotiation ninja!

Chapter 45: Future Trends in Supplier Relationship Management

Welcome to Chapter 45 of "Strike Deals Like a Pro: Unleash Your Inner Negotiation Ninja and Command Supplier Success." In this chapter, we'll explore emerging trends and future directions in supplier relationship management (SRM) that are shaping the way organizations engage with their suppliers and drive value from their supply chains.

Here's what we'll cover in this chapter:

1. Digital transformation in SRM: Delve into the ongoing digital transformation of SRM practices driven by

advancements in technology, such as artificial intelligence (AI), machine learning (ML), blockchain, and the Internet of Things (IoT). Learn how these technologies are revolutionizing SRM processes and enabling organizations to achieve greater efficiency, agility, and innovation in their supplier relationships.
2. Supplier collaboration and co-innovation: Explore the growing emphasis on supplier collaboration and co-innovation as organizations seek to leverage the expertise and capabilities of their suppliers to drive product innovation, process improvement, and competitive advantage. Learn how collaborative partnerships with suppliers can foster creativity, agility, and value creation throughout the supply chain.
3. Sustainability and ESG considerations: Understand the increasing importance of sustainability and environmental, social, and governance (ESG) considerations in SRM practices. Learn how organizations are integrating

sustainability criteria into supplier selection, evaluation, and performance management processes to mitigate risk, enhance reputation, and drive positive social and environmental impact.
4. Supply chain resilience and risk management: Delve into the growing focus on supply chain resilience and risk management in response to increasing global uncertainties, disruptions, and geopolitical tensions. Learn how organizations are adopting proactive approaches to identify, assess, and mitigate supply chain risks, build redundancy and flexibility into their supply chains, and enhance their ability to respond to unexpected events.
5. Ethical and responsible sourcing: Explore the rising consumer and regulatory demand for ethical and responsible sourcing practices, including fair labor practices, human rights protection, and supply chain transparency. Learn how organizations are implementing ethical

sourcing initiatives and leveraging technology to trace and verify the origin and authenticity of products throughout the supply chain.

6. Agile and adaptive SRM practices: Delve into the importance of agility and adaptability in SRM practices to respond to changing market dynamics, customer preferences, and competitive pressures. Learn how organizations are adopting agile methodologies, flexible contract structures, and dynamic supplier relationships to navigate uncertainty and drive business resilience.

Throughout this chapter, we'll explore how these emerging trends and future directions are reshaping the landscape of supplier relationship management and providing new opportunities for organizations to create value, drive innovation, and build sustainable, resilient supply chains. By staying ahead of the curve and embracing these trends, you'll position your organization for success in an increasingly complex and interconnected business environment. So, let's dive in and uncover the future of supplier relationship management like a negotiation ninja!

Chapter 46: The Role of Trust in Supplier Relationships

Welcome to Chapter 46 of "Strike Deals Like a Pro: Unleash Your Inner Negotiation Ninja and Command Supplier Success." In this chapter, we'll explore the pivotal role of trust in supplier relationships and how it serves as the foundation for successful collaboration, innovation, and long-term partnerships.

Here's what we'll cover in this chapter:

1. Understanding the importance of trust: Delve into why trust is essential in supplier relationships and how it contributes to effective collaboration, communication, and problem-solving. Learn how trust fosters transparency, reliability, and mutual

respect between buyers and suppliers, laying the groundwork for successful partnerships.
2. Building trust with suppliers: Explore strategies for building trust with your suppliers through consistent, honest, and reliable behavior. Learn how to fulfill commitments, communicate openly, and demonstrate integrity in your interactions to earn the trust and confidence of your suppliers.
3. Communication and transparency: Understand the role of communication and transparency in building trust with suppliers. Learn how to share information openly, provide feedback constructively, and address issues promptly and transparently to foster trust and collaboration.
4. Reliability and consistency: Delve into the importance of reliability and consistency in building trust with suppliers. Learn how to deliver on your promises, meet expectations consistently, and demonstrate reliability in your actions and decisions to

instill confidence and trust in your supplier relationships.
5. Conflict resolution and problem-solving: Explore how trust facilitates conflict resolution and problem-solving in supplier relationships. Learn how to navigate disagreements, resolve conflicts, and find mutually acceptable solutions through open dialogue, empathy, and trust-building behaviors.
6. Cultivating a trust-based culture: Delve into strategies for cultivating a trust-based culture within your organization and across your supply chain. Learn how to lead by example, empower employees to make decisions, and foster a culture of accountability, transparency, and collaboration to strengthen trust and relationships with suppliers.

Throughout this chapter, we'll delve into real-world examples, case studies, and practical exercises to help you understand the importance of trust in supplier relationships and develop strategies for building and maintaining trust with your suppliers. By prioritizing trust in your supplier relationships, you'll create a solid foundation for collaboration, innovation, and long-term success in your business endeavors. So, let's dive in and uncover the secrets to building trust like a negotiation ninja!

Chapter 47: Cultural Intelligence in Global Supplier Relationships

Welcome to Chapter 47 of "Strike Deals Like a Pro: Unleash Your Inner Negotiation Ninja and Command Supplier Success." In this chapter, we'll explore the concept of cultural intelligence (CQ) and its importance in building effective relationships with global suppliers across diverse cultural contexts.

Here's what we'll cover in this chapter:

1. Understanding cultural intelligence: Delve into the concept of cultural intelligence (CQ) and its significance in navigating cultural differences and fostering

successful interactions with suppliers from diverse cultural backgrounds. Learn how CQ encompasses the knowledge, skills, and attitudes needed to adapt and work effectively across cultures.
2. Cultural awareness and sensitivity: Explore strategies for developing cultural awareness and sensitivity in supplier relationships. Learn how to recognize and respect cultural differences in communication styles, business practices, and social norms to avoid misunderstandings and build rapport with suppliers from different cultural backgrounds.
3. Cross-cultural communication: Understand the importance of effective cross-cultural communication in global supplier relationships. Learn how to adapt your communication style, language, and nonverbal cues to bridge cultural gaps, convey messages clearly, and establish trust and rapport with suppliers across cultural boundaries.

4. Building trust and rapport: Delve into how cultural intelligence contributes to building trust and rapport with global suppliers. Learn how to demonstrate respect for cultural differences, show genuine interest in understanding your suppliers' perspectives, and adapt your behavior to align with cultural norms and expectations.
5. Negotiating across cultures: Explore strategies for negotiating successfully with suppliers from diverse cultural backgrounds. Learn how to adapt your negotiation approach, understand cultural preferences for decision-making, and build relationships based on trust, reciprocity, and mutual respect to achieve mutually beneficial outcomes.
6. Managing cultural differences: Delve into techniques for managing cultural differences and resolving conflicts that may arise in global supplier relationships. Learn how to navigate cultural differences in decision-making, problem-solving, and conflict resolution to maintain positive relationships and achieve shared goals.

Throughout this chapter, we'll delve into real-world examples, case studies, and practical exercises to help you develop cultural intelligence and navigate cultural differences effectively in global supplier relationships. By cultivating cultural intelligence and embracing diversity in your supplier relationships, you'll enhance your ability to collaborate across cultures, drive innovation, and achieve success in the global marketplace. So, let's dive in and uncover the secrets to cultural intelligence like a negotiation ninja!

Chapter 48: The Future of Sustainable Procurement

Welcome to Chapter 48 of "Strike Deals Like a Pro: Unleash Your Inner Negotiation Ninja and Command Supplier Success." In this chapter, we'll explore the future of sustainable procurement and the evolving trends and practices shaping the sustainability agenda in supplier relationships.

Here's what we'll cover in this chapter:

1. Sustainable procurement as a strategic imperative: Delve into why sustainable procurement is increasingly viewed as a strategic imperative for organizations seeking to address environmental, social, and economic challenges while driving value and innovation in their supply chains.
2. Circular economy and closed-loop supply chains: Explore the growing adoption of circular economy principles and closed-loop supply chain models in sustainable procurement practices. Learn how organizations are redesigning products, materials, and processes to minimize waste, maximize resource efficiency, and promote circularity throughout the product lifecycle.
3. Supply chain transparency and traceability: Understand the importance

of supply chain transparency and traceability in sustainable procurement efforts. Learn how organizations are leveraging technology, such as blockchain and digital traceability solutions, to track and verify the origin, authenticity, and sustainability credentials of products and materials throughout the supply chain.

4. Ethical and responsible sourcing: Delve into the continued focus on ethical and responsible sourcing practices in sustainable procurement. Learn how organizations are implementing ethical sourcing initiatives, conducting due diligence on suppliers, and promoting fair labor practices, human rights protection, and responsible business conduct throughout their supply chains.

5. Climate resilience and adaptation: Explore the growing emphasis on climate resilience and adaptation in sustainable procurement strategies. Learn how organizations are assessing

climate risks, integrating climate considerations into supplier selection and evaluation processes, and collaborating with suppliers to reduce greenhouse gas emissions, mitigate climate impacts, and build resilience to climate-related disruptions.

6. Stakeholder engagement and collaboration: Understand the importance of stakeholder engagement and collaboration in advancing sustainable procurement goals. Learn how organizations are partnering with suppliers, customers, investors, and civil society organizations to set ambitious sustainability targets, drive innovation, and create shared value throughout the supply chain.

Throughout this chapter, we'll delve into real-world examples, case studies, and emerging practices to help you envision the future of sustainable procurement and position your organization as a leader in sustainable supply chain management. By embracing sustainable procurement practices and collaborating with stakeholders, you'll enhance your organization's resilience, competitiveness, and positive impact on society and the environment. So, let's dive in and uncover the future of sustainable procurement like a negotiation ninja!

Chapter 49: Supplier Relationship Governance Frameworks

Welcome to Chapter 49 of "Strike Deals Like a Pro: Unleash Your Inner Negotiation Ninja and Command Supplier Success." In this chapter, we'll explore the importance of supplier relationship governance frameworks and how they provide structure and oversight to supplier relationships to ensure alignment with business objectives and drive value creation.

Here's what we'll cover in this chapter:

1. Introduction to supplier relationship governance: Delve into the concept of supplier relationship governance and its role in managing and optimizing supplier relationships. Learn how supplier relationship governance frameworks provide the structure, processes, and mechanisms needed to effectively govern supplier relationships and achieve desired outcomes.
2. Key components of supplier relationship governance frameworks: Explore the key components of supplier relationship governance frameworks, including governance structures, roles and responsibilities, performance metrics, communication protocols, and escalation procedures. Learn how these components work together to establish

clear expectations, accountability, and alignment with business goals.
3. Establishing governance structures: Understand the importance of establishing governance structures tailored to the complexity and strategic importance of supplier relationships. Learn how to define governance roles, establish cross-functional governance teams, and allocate responsibilities for supplier management, oversight, and decision-making.
4. Defining performance metrics and KPIs: Delve into the process of defining performance metrics and key performance indicators (KPIs) to measure supplier performance and track progress towards strategic objectives. Learn how to establish SMART (Specific, Measurable, Achievable, Relevant, Time-bound) metrics aligned with business priorities and supplier capabilities.
5. Implementing communication and reporting mechanisms: Explore

strategies for implementing communication and reporting mechanisms to facilitate transparency, collaboration, and accountability in supplier relationships. Learn how to establish regular communication channels, conduct performance reviews, and report on supplier performance to stakeholders.

6. Continuous improvement and adaptation: Understand the importance of continuous improvement and adaptation in supplier relationship governance. Learn how to review and evaluate governance frameworks regularly, solicit feedback from stakeholders, and adapt governance practices based on lessons learned and changing business needs.

Throughout this chapter, we'll delve into real-world examples, case studies, and practical insights to help you develop and implement effective supplier relationship governance frameworks. By establishing clear governance structures, defining performance metrics, and fostering collaboration and accountability in supplier relationships, you'll enhance your organization's ability to drive value, mitigate risk, and achieve strategic objectives through supplier partnerships. So, let's dive in and uncover the secrets to supplier relationship governance like a negotiation ninja!

Chapter 50: Supplier Relationship Exit Strategies

Welcome to Chapter 50 of "Strike Deals Like a Pro: Unleash Your Inner Negotiation Ninja and Command Supplier Success." In this final chapter, we'll explore the often overlooked but critical aspect of supplier relationship exits strategies and how organizations can effectively manage the end of supplier relationships while mitigating risk and preserving value.

Here's what we'll cover in this chapter:

1. Understanding supplier relationship exits: Delve into the reasons why organizations may need to terminate or transition supplier relationships, including performance issues, changes in business needs, market dynamics, and strategic shifts. Learn why it's essential to plan for and execute supplier exits strategically and responsibly.
2. Risk assessment and contingency planning: Explore strategies for assessing and

mitigating risks associated with supplier relationship exits. Learn how to identify potential risks, such as supply chain disruptions, quality issues, contractual obligations, and reputational risks, and develop contingency plans to address them proactively.
3. Contractual considerations and obligations: Understand the importance of reviewing contractual terms and obligations when planning a supplier relationship exit. Learn how to assess contract termination clauses, notice periods, exit procedures, and any potential financial or legal implications associated with ending the supplier relationship.
4. Transition planning and execution: Delve into the process of planning and executing supplier relationship transitions smoothly and efficiently. Learn how to develop transition plans, communicate effectively with suppliers and stakeholders, transfer knowledge and responsibilities, and minimize disruptions to business operations.
5. Managing stakeholder relationships: Explore strategies for managing stakeholder relationships throughout the supplier

relationship exit process. Learn how to communicate transparently with internal and external stakeholders, address concerns and questions, and maintain trust and confidence in your organization's ability to manage supplier transitions effectively.

6. Post-exit evaluation and lessons learned: Understand the importance of conducting post-exit evaluations and capturing lessons learned to improve future supplier relationship management practices. Learn how to analyze the outcomes of supplier exits, identify areas for improvement, and implement changes to enhance your organization's approach to supplier relationship management.

Throughout this chapter, we'll delve into real-world examples, case studies, and practical insights to help you develop effective supplier relationship exit strategies and ensure a smooth and responsible transition when ending supplier relationships. By proactively planning for supplier exits and managing them strategically, you'll minimize risk, protect value, and maintain positive relationships with suppliers and stakeholders. So, let's dive in and uncover the secrets to supplier relationship exits like a negotiation ninja!

www.ingramcontent.com/pod-product-compliance
Lightning Source LLC
Chambersburg PA
CBHW050101230526
45470CB00004B/1627